"According to *Follow the Lamb,* the book of Revelation foc⏀ [...]
the future but on transformation in the present. Anyone ⏀ [...]
'crown jewel of the Bible' should put down everything else [...]
From 'the golden ticket' for understanding Revelation—that it is about Jesus above all
else—to the 'wild world of apocalypses,' he expertly and sensitively introduces key insights (prerequisites) for grasping the intended meaning of the Bible's grand finale. Those
who read the book of Revelation through the lenses provided in his book will be better
prepared than ever to 'follow the Lamb.'"

—BRENT SANDY, Adjunct Professor of New Testament, Wheaton College;
Professor and Chair, Department of Religious Studies, Grace College (retired)

"I enthusiastically recommend Dalrymple's book *Follow the Lamb.* I have read all
of Dalrymple's books, and this one, without question, is one of his best. His ability to
explain the text of Revelation with clarity and concision while maintaining a sound
hermeneutical methodology and a robust theology all while maintaining pastoral sensitively is truly impressive. In this book, Dalrymple offers several keys for understanding the message of Revelation while avoiding the pitfalls of tunnel vision, ax grinding,
and excessive speculations. He points the reader to what the text actually says as he
opens up vistas showcasing the beauty and grandeur of Revelation in a panoramic framework enabling one see how the parts fit within the whole. He masterfully manages to
transform the kaleidoscopic imagery of John's vision into a telescope by which to view
the glory of God, the victory of Christ, and the destiny of the people of God arrayed
in splendor. As a professor who regularly reads, writes, and teaches on Revelation, I find
that Dalrymple's book strikes the right balance between hermeneutics and exposition.
It represents what I look for when selecting a textbook for my students. While it is not
a comprehensive introduction or commentary on Revelation, it is one of the of the most
accessible explanations of what good hermeneutics looks like and how it relates to the
theology, themes, and message of this climactic book of prophecy."

—ALAN S. BANDY, Rowena R. Strickland Associate Professor of
New Testament and Greek, Oklahoma Baptist University

"I often tell my students that the New Testament is ultimately an extended commentary
on the Old that focuses on two things: Christ and following Christ (Christology and
costly discipleship). With passion and clarity, Dalrymple demonstrates that this is true
also for Revelation. His insightful book will illuminate much else about Revelation that
is often misunderstood and misapplied. It deserves a wide readership."

—MICHAEL J. GORMAN, Raymond E. Brown Professor of Biblical Studies and Theology,
St. Mary's Seminary and University

"Dalrymple's *Follow the Lamb* is a wise and trustworthy contribution to understanding
one of the New Testament's most mysterious books. Dalrymple immerses readers in the
text of Revelation from the beginning and his multi-level approach allows them to go
as deep as their interests will carry them. He provides helpful overviews of the structure
of the book along with exploring its literary and theological themes. Readers will also
be extremely interested in the contemporary issues that continually surface throughout
Follow the Lamb (e.g., justice, holy war, popular readings). I predict this book will serve
as an introductory guide in many college and seminary classrooms, the book of choice

in Bible study groups and church small groups, as well as a good read for individuals interested in all things apocalyptic."

—J. Scott Duvall, Chair, Department of Biblical Studies, Ouachita Baptist University

"Christians uniformly agree that Revelation is the most difficult book in the Bible to understand. Dalrymple provides a readable and reliable guide to help readers negotiate John's apocalyptic visions. His primary and secondary keys provide interpretative entry points to comprehend and apply the text. Revelation is also the most controversial of biblical books, and Dalrymple addresses some common abuses found in popular interpretations. His volume will both inform and challenge those with ears to hear in the church today."

—Mark Wilson, Founder and Director, Asia Minor Research Center, Turkey

FOLLOW
the
LAMB

ROB DALRYMPLE

FOLLOW *the* LAMB

A Guide to Reading,

Understanding, and Applying

the Book of Revelation

WEAVER BOOK
COMPANY
WOOSTER, OHIO

Follow the Lamb: A Guide to Reading, Understanding, and Applying the Book of Revelation
© 2017 by Rob Dalrymple

Published by
Weaver Book Company
1190 Summerset Dr.
Wooster, OH 44691
Visit us at weaverbookcompany.com

Scriptural references in parentheses that are from the book of Revelation include only the chapter and verse(s). When Scriptural citations in parentheses reference books other than Revelation, the citation includes book, chapter, and verse(s).

Scripture quotations are from the New American Standard Bible®. Copyright © 1960, 1962, 1963, 1968, 1971, 1972, 1973, 1975, 1977, 1995 by The Lockman Foundation. Used by permission. www.Lockman.org.

All Scripture quotations, unless otherwise indicated, are from the New American Standard Bible®. Copyright © 1960, 1962, 1963, 1968, 1971, 1972, 1973, 1975, 1977, 1995 by The Lockman Foundation. Used by permission. www.Lockman.org.

Cover: Frank Gutbrod
Interior Design: Nicholas Richardson

Print: 978-1-941337-94-3
EPUB: 978-1-941337-95-0

Library of Congress Cataloging-in-Publication Data
A CIP catalogue record for this book is available from the Library of Congress.

Printed in the United States of America

I dedicate this book to my children:
Justin, Jordan, Jared, and McKenzie.
I pray that I have been faithful in following the Lamb,
and in doing so have modeled what it means to
imitate Jesus for you. I am very proud of you.
May you continue to follow the Lamb
wherever He leads!

Contents

Prologue. 11
Acknowledgments. 15
Introduction: Why You Should Master the Book of Revelation 17

Part 1: Primary Keys for Reading, Understanding, and Applying the Book of Revelation
Introduction to Part 1 27
Chapter 1: Christ in the Book of Revelation 29
Chapter 2: The People of God as Imitators of Christ. 38
Chapter 3: "Overcome": Revelation's Most Important Word. . . . 45
Chapter 4: Imagery and the Old Testament 54
Conclusion to Part 1 64

Part 2: Secondary Keys to Reading Revelation Effectively
Introduction to Part 2. 69
Chapter 5: John's Use of Numbers 71
Chapter 6: Understanding Genre and Revelation 85
Conclusion to Part 2. 96

Part 3: Reading Revelation as Literature
Introduction to Part 3 101
Chapter 7: Inclusios: Structure and the Book of Revelation . . . 105
Chapter 8: Repetition: Structure and the Book of Revelation . . 112
Chapter 9: Reading Revelation as a Story 124
Conclusion to Part 3. 134

Part 4: Issues and Themes in the Book of Revelation
Introduction to Part 4. 137
Chapter 10: Revelation and Dualism 139
Chapter 11: Revelation and Symbolism. 147

Chapter 12: Revelation and Holy War .153
Chapter 13: Revelation and Justice 161
Conclusion to Part 4 170

Epilogue 171
Appendix 1: Symbolism and the Popular Understanding
    of Revelation 173
Appendix 2: The Nature of Language in Scripture in
    General and Prophecy in Particular 175
Appendix 3: Evangelicals and Armageddon 180
Appendix 4: Is Revelation about the End of the World? 185
Bibliography 187

Prologue

Revelation is arguably one of the greatest pieces of literature in the history of the world and one of the great books within the Bible. Unfortunately, for many the book of Revelation remains a mystery, which few dare to explore. Ironically, the book opens with a blessing for its reader, hearers, and keepers (1:3).[1] This raises the question: How can one be blessed by reading a book that no one seems to understand?

Early in my academic years this question troubled me. As a young man, I had concluded that Revelation was a mystery that would only be solved after everything was over. And I gave up trying to understand it.

Now you must understand that in my younger days I was fascinated with the "end times" and all of the hype that went along with it. I grew up in the 70s (I was born in 666—no, really, June of 1966). At this time, the evangelical fascination was high regarding world events and their apparent proof that the fulfillment of everything was right at the door. I read dozens of books and endeavored to discern how everything was being fulfilled right before our eyes. I even spent hours in a local library one day to determine if there really was an increase in the number and frequency of earthquakes in the last century—after all, I was convinced that this would have been a clear sign of the imminent return of Christ!

But problems began to surface for me along two fronts. First, I began to observe that there were tremendous disagreements among the popular writers regarding both the meaning of the book of Revelation in particular

---

1. This book uses the following convention for Scriptural references: When citations in parentheses are from the book of Revelation, only chapter and verse(s) are used; when citations in parentheses come from outside of Revelation, they include book, chapter, and verse(s).

and the end times in general. I felt an uneasiness in my heart as I grappled with these things. Who should I trust? The second problem was that none of them seemed to have it correct. Nothing they said would happen came true. They seemed to do well when it came to the past. But when it came to the present and the immediate future, time proved them wrong.

My disillusionment grew throughout the 80s. Many of the prophecies that I had been confident were being fulfilled among us never seemed to actually come to pass. Then in 1989 when the Berlin Wall fell and the Iron Curtain was beginning to be dismantled, I became totally disillusioned. Things were clearly not unfolding as I had been told by the so-called prophecy experts.[2]

The problem was more than the fact that prophecies were not being fulfilled as I had come to expect. The problem was that things were moving in the opposite direction from what I had come to believe. Armageddon was supposed to happen in the 1980s. Yet it became more and more evident that the Soviets were not about to invade Israel, nor the Middle East.

It was in this state of disillusionment that I concluded that the book of Revelation was a mystery not to be understood by human beings. Though I continued to study the Scriptures and to refine my understanding of eschatology and the New Testament (NT), I decided that the book of Revelation was off-limits. I envisioned that there should be a blank page in my Bible before the book of Revelation (like what one finds between the end of Malachi, the last book of the Old Testament [OT], and the beginning of Matthew, the first book of the NT). This blank page needed to read: Do Not Trespass.

Mind you, my convictions about not reading or being able to understand the book of Revelation did not sit comfortably with me. I knew the promise that all Scripture, which included the book of Revelation, was "profitable for teaching, for reproof, for correction, for training in righteousness" (2 Tim. 3:16).[3] I was also aware of the fact that the book of

---

2. What baffles my mind and troubles my heart today is that many of these same so-called prophecy experts are still writing books. They have changed their script. And they seemingly have garnered a whole new audience. I want to shout sometimes, "Don't listen to them; they were wrong the last time!"

3. I recognize that in context 2 Timothy 3:16 is referring to the OT. But I also recognize that in the canon of Scripture, which the NT has been incorporated into, the assurance of 2 Timothy 3:16 may be applied to the book of Revelation also.

Revelation opens with a promise of blessing for its readers, hearers, and keepers (1:3). Somehow, this book was meant to be read, studied, and used by the church. Yet it made no sense. How could anyone do what it says when no one knows what it means?

The Lord, of course, has a way of messing with us. He knew I had a passion for Scripture. I soon found myself pursuing graduate and post graduate studies in the NT. I decided on my own to renew my studies in the book of Revelation and I soon ventured into several standard evangelical commentaries. It was not long before I realized that there was a significant amount of agreement among a wide range of scholars (including conservative evangelicals) regarding the book of Revelation. And I quickly began to fall in love with the message of the book of Revelation.

I found that the message of the book of Revelation was first and foremost about Jesus. This was not hard to see, after all, the first verse begins with "the revelation of Jesus Christ" (1:1). This alone should be enough for every Christian to be consumed with studying. But as I soon found out, there was more. And this *more* relates to every follower of Christ.

The goal of this book is to introduce the reader to the fundamental principles for reading, understanding, and applying the book of Revelation today. So if you have ever been disillusioned with the book of Revelation, or just wanted to learn what it means, I invite you to explore the wonders and marvels of this great piece of literature. Come on! Let's learn to "follow the Lamb wherever He goes" (14:4).

Rob Dalrymple
March 2017

Acknowledgments

I would like to thank Ian Spencer for his kind and helpful corrections to my attempts at putting something cogent together. Ian is a great thinker, communicator, and friend. Your help has made this book readable for everyone else and for that I (and they) am greatful (I thought I would have one typo that you missed!).

I would like to thank my students over the years who have allowed me to teach endlessly about the book of Revelation. You have allowed me to pursue my passion for this book and to justify it by teaching you. I only pray that it has been as profitable for you as it has been for me.

Why You Should Master the Book of Revelation

My son texted me the other day: "Dad, what view of Revelation do you support?" He was asking because it was the last day of his New Testament Survey course and his professor was providing an overview of the book of Revelation. Herein lies one of the problems for understanding the book of Revelation in the twenty-first-century church: Many of our pastors and leaders are simply not given adequate training on how to interpret the book of Revelation.

For most pastors and church leaders their exposure to the book of Revelation is often confined to one lecture, or a portion of a lecture, during the last day of class—along with any modest reading the professor may have assigned.[1] The problem is exacerbated by the fact that these pastors often end up in local congregations where there always seems to be a few members who have studied the book of Revelation and eschatology (the study of the end times). These well-meaning churchgoers have often been influenced by the popular literature that pervades the Christian marketplace. Unfortunately, this literature, which does not reflect the convictions of many (if not most) within the scholarly world, often does more harm than good.

Why is it, then, that pastors tend to shy away from preaching from the book of Revelation? After all, they are not necessarily any more equipped

---

1. This is often the case for those who attend seminary, though it is much worse for those who only have a college degree. Dare we even speak of the trend among many evangelicals to hire pastors who have no formal theological training?

with the meaning of Hebrews, James, Ruth, or Malachi, yet they do not shy from preaching on these books. The simple answer is that most pastors believe that preaching on the book of Revelation may well cause too many problems. They are not concerned about upsetting deeply held convictions on the end of the world when they preach from Hebrews, James, Ruth, or Malachi. Revelation, on the other hand, represents deep waters that many are not willing to tread. The unintended consequence of this is that these popular convictions continue to spread unhindered in the local church.

This book is intended to provide schools and churches with a tool that one can navigate through to find the beauty and richness of this magnificent and significantly important part of Scripture. The goal is to introduce key principles that will aid you in reading, understanding, and applying the book of Revelation.

We will take baby steps. First, we will learn how to read the book of Revelation in light of Jesus. Then, we will incrementally increase our ability to understand the book of Revelation well.

Each chapter is intentionally brief, though some are briefer than others. Each one will close with a For Further Study section. These questions are vital. Many of the questions will allow you to go further in your study and process what you have learned.

Some of the questions in the For Further Study sections may require some deep reflection. Take the time to do so. It will only add to your appreciation of the beauty of the book and its message. At other points, you will be encouraged to read and reread the book of Revelation. Again, take the time to do so.

The book of Revelation is one of the most rewarding books to study in all Scripture. As we will learn, it was meant to be read, reread, and reread again. And it is worth our study. After all, we are told that if we read and do what is says we are blessed: "Blessed is he who reads and those who hear the words of the prophecy, and heed the things which are written in it; for the time is near" (1:3).[2]

John intended for us to do much more than just read. He wanted us to explore. And each step of our journey will take us deeper and deeper into

---

2. Unless otherwise noted, all translations of Scripture are from the New American Standard Bible (NASB).

the profound mysteries of Jesus, His call for His people, and the ultimate triumph of the gospel.

To be blessed for "heed[ing] the things which are written in the book," we face one obstacle: we must understand what the book means and discern how to apply it to our lives. This is our goal: to learn to interpret the book of Revelation in light of its original meaning so that we might learn to apply its message to our lives and thus more faithfully "follow the Lamb wherever He goes" (14:4).

THE NATURE OF THIS STUDY

One of the difficulties most students of the book of Revelation encounter is navigating through all the different interpretive issues in the book of Revelation. Most introductions to the book of Revelation have page after page introducing the reader to the myriad difficulties in Revelation.

This study intends to be different. Instead of spending chapter after chapter introducing Revelation, which often bogs the reader down so much they never get into the text itself and tends to leave the reader more confused than when they started, this book aims to help the readers explore the book of Revelation one step at a time.

In Part 1, we will examine the book of Revelation and observe that there are only two keys to understanding its primary message. The first key is that the book is about Jesus. Right from the beginning we learn that it is "the Revelation of Jesus Christ" (1:1). The significance of this fact is that all Christians can agree on it! We can all rejoice and celebrate the incredible message of Jesus as the Lamb of God who has overcome (5:5–6). We do not have to worry about charts or schemes or assumptions or anything. For John, and the rest of the NT for that matter, Jesus is the key to understanding the Scriptures.

The second key is that the language and images used by John throughout the book of Revelation derive from the OT. Though many get caught up in the mire of John's imagery and the exhaustive efforts to discern what all the symbols mean, our efforts will be greatly simplified once we discern that John's imagery comes from the OT.

If all we take from our study of Revelation is an ability to understand the book in light of these two keys, we will be much better off. But it is here that we may wish to add an additional point: By combining these two keys, we see not only that the book of Revelation is about Jesus but more specifically how God's promises in the OT have been fulfilled in Jesus.

This is what makes Revelation so great—the message is all about Jesus. In the Gospels, we have a description of the life and times of Jesus of Nazareth. We are indeed told that He was the eternal Son of God in human flesh. But to some extent we might say that His glory was veiled during His life and ministry on earth. Certainly, we get glimpses of Jesus' glorious nature in events like the transfiguration. But overall it is the humanity of Christ that shines through. In Acts and the Letters of the NT, we see references to Christ's life and work, especially the cross and resurrection. In the Epistles, Paul and the apostles provide us with great theological statements concerning Jesus' true identity.[3]

It is in the book of Revelation, however, that we get this tremendous picture of the glory of the resurrected Christ. We see what it means for God to have answered Jesus' request in John 17 to give Him His glory again. Note, for example, Revelation's opening description of Jesus:

> Then I turned to see the voice that was speaking with me. And having turned I saw seven golden lampstands; and in the middle of the lampstands I saw one like a son of man, clothed in a robe reaching to the feet, and girded across His chest with a golden sash. His head and His hair were white like white wool, like snow; and His eyes were like a flame of fire. His feet were like burnished bronze, when it has been made to glow in a furnace, and His voice was like the sound of many waters. In His right hand He held seven stars, and out of His mouth came a sharp two-edged sword; and His face was like the sun shining in its strength. When I saw Him, I fell at His feet like a dead man. And He placed His right hand on me, saying, "Do not be afraid; I am the first and the last, and the living One; and I was dead, and behold, I am alive forevermore, and I have the keys of death and of Hades." (1:12–18)

The greatness of the story of Revelation is that it does not end there. There is one more significant aspect of interpreting the book of Revelation that we must get our heads around. For John, the author of the book of

---

3. For example, Philippians 2:5–11 and Colossians 1:15–20.

Revelation (1:9), the story of Jesus has an important message for the people of God, both then and now—namely, that the people of God must emulate Jesus and faithfully proclaim the kingdom of God, even to the point of death. That is, we are called to "follow the Lamb wherever He goes" (14:4).

THE PURPOSE OF THIS BOOK

This book is not a standard introduction on how to read the book of Revelation. Many helpful commentaries and introductory resources on the book of Revelation begin with an elaborate overview on the nature of apocalyptic writings, an explanation of the various views of interpretation, the possible backgrounds and settings of the book, and other such explanatory sections.

The goal of this book is to discern how to read, understand, and apply the book of Revelation. My approach will be more inductive. We will simply begin with the surface level of the text: looking primarily at Revelation's depiction of the person and work of Christ. As we venture forward, we will continue to dig more deeply into the book of Revelation. Each step of the way will expand on what we have already learned.

DISCERNING THE AUTHOR'S INTENT

As students of the Bible, our goal in reading the Scriptures is to discern what the text means for us today: What can I learn from this text that will affect what I believe and how I am supposed to live my Christian life? In order to answer these questions, it is necessary to discern what the text meant at the time it was written—both to the author who wrote it and for his readers. Only after determining this may we ask what it means for us today. If we could discern John's intent for writing the book—that is, what he was trying to convey to God's people and why—we would make great strides in ascertaining what the book means for us today. Our goal in this study is to learn how to read and understand the book of Revelation in order that we might begin to discern what it means and how it applies to today.

OVERVIEW OF THIS BOOK

In Part 1, I lay out the primary elements of John's message. In chapter 1, we will see that the first key to understanding the book of Revelation is that it is about Jesus. This is the golden ticket. If we read Revelation and gain only one thing from it, may it be that we see the exalted status of our glorified, risen Lord. The beauty here is that everyone can agree on this.

Then over the next two chapters, we will build on our understanding of Jesus by observing John's depiction of the mission of the people of God. In chapter 2, we will see that the reason why it is so important to discern the book of Revelation's depiction of Jesus is that the people of God are called to imitate Jesus.

In chapter 3 we will examine John's primary exhortation to his readers—namely, that they are to overcome. We will see that the people of God, who are called to carry forth the mission of Christ, must also know that this task will be difficult and will require perseverance. Here again, we will see that John's appeal to overcome is grounded in Christ: "He who overcomes, I will grant to him to sit down with Me on My throne, as I also overcame and sat down with My Father on His throne" (3:21).

Chapter 4 will bring Part 1 to a close. Here we will examine the second key to reading and understanding Revelation—namely, that the abundant imagery that John uses throughout the book derives from the OT. That is, John is reading the story of Jesus and the people of God from the perspective that all of God's promises throughout the OT are fulfilled in Jesus.

In Part 2 we will begin to discern some of the incredible ways in which John has carefully written the book of Revelation. A close reading of the book will confirm that John has quite intentionally constructed Revelation in such a way that discerning readers may continue to unveil new levels of depth and beauty.

Chapter 5 will examine John's use of numbers. When I refer to John's use of numbers, I mean not just his use of explicit numbers themselves (such as 666), but also the fact that a significant amount of words and phrases occur three, four, seven, or twelve times; and even multiples of these numbers (such as 28: 7 x 4; 24: 12 + 12; or 144: 12 x 12). Because these numbers are used with great frequency and consistency throughout Revelation, the most reasonable conclusion is that John has done this intentionally. Understanding John's use of numbers, therefore, will not only confirm the beauty of this book but will enhance our understanding of its message.

Chapter 6 will unpack the three main genres, or styles of writing, in the book of Revelation. Revelation combines apocalyptic, epistolary, and prophetic styles. Learning to interpret the book of Revelation will require an awareness of ancient letters, prophecy, and the wild world of apocalypses—as well as how John integrates all three of these.

In Part 3 we will continue to delve more deeply into understanding the book of Revelation. In this part we will begin to examine the structure of Revelation. We will observe how John uses repetition as a means of aiding his readers.

In chapter 7 we will see that John uses an ancient practice called inclusio to help his readers (or "hearers"). An inclusio is a literary feature in which an author will repeat a key expression to mark the beginning and the end of a unit. That is, where a modern author might use a paragraph or chapter break, ancient authors would use repetition. Discerning John's use of inclusios will aid greatly in our ability to interpret the book of Revelation.

In chapter 8 we will examine John's use of repetition. It appears that there are certain items that John wants us to know and focus on. He makes this clear by his use of repetition. Here again, we see the depth and beauty of Revelation. Learning to observe how John has intricately written his book will enhance our ability to discern the meaning of Revelation.

In chapter 9 we will look briefly at the nature of the narrative of Revelation. Though it may be difficult at first glance to discern, the book of Revelation is telling a story. This story expands and unfolds as it develops. Again, the beauty of Revelation is uncovered as we see how John develops his narrative. It is essential to discern the larger plot that resides within the book of Revelation in order to learn to interpret it well.

Our study will conclude in Part 4. Here we will examine a few additional (and often overlooked) themes. We will begin in chapter 10 by examining the nature of dualism and its importance. We will see how Revelation features a number of dualities: the people of God and the nations, Christ and the beast, and the bride and the harlot. Recognizing John's use of such dualism is significant for understanding some of the more complex questions that arise today.

Chapter 11 will take a more complete look at the question of symbolism. In many ways, the issue of symbolism will already have been addressed throughout our study. At this point, we will confirm that John has indeed used symbolism throughout his writing. We will examine the importance of this for our interpreting the book of Revelation today.

Chapter 12 will examine another overlooked theme that undergirds John's narrative—namely, John's use of holy war. The theme of holy war, which is present in several biblical writings, provides another important backdrop for understanding the book of Revelation.

The issue of holy war raises another important theme in the book of Revelation—namely, the notion of justice, which we will examine in chapter 13. Ironically, though modern readers might often struggle with the question of justice and God's wrath upon the nations, we will observe that for John and his readers the question of justice focused primarily on the question of when God would bring relief for His people.

In all, the book of Revelation is the crown jewel of the Bible. Unfortunately it is often ignored or misunderstood. Our goal is to lay a foundation upon which you may learn to read, understand, and apply this wonderful text. "Blessed" indeed are those who "read" and those who "hear" and those who "heed the things that are written in it" because "the time is near" (1:3).

PART 1

Primary Keys for Reading, Understanding, and Applying the Book of Revelation

Introduction to Part 1

The message of the book of Revelation may be summed up as follows: Since Jesus is the "faithful witness" (1:5), and the Lion/Lamb who has overcome (5:5–6), then the people of God are to follow the Lamb. Simply put, the book of Revelation is an exhortation for the people of God to follow the Lamb. It is a manifesto of sorts. In this manifesto, God's people are called to carry forth the testimony of Christ to the nations.

This mission will not be without its challenges. There will be challenges from without—namely, opposition that takes the form of persecution. And there will be challenges from within—most notably, false teachers who will endeavor to lead the people of God astray. In the end, those who faithfully follow the Lamb and overcome all that opposes them will dine with Him in His eternal kingdom.

This part of our study will set forth two primary keys to effectively reading, understanding, and applying the book of Revelation.

CHAPTER 1

Christ in the Book of Revelation

Christ is the center of the Apocalypse.[1] Or perhaps it may be better stated: Christ *is* the Apocalypse. Author Paul Minear notes, "When one asks where, in the first eight verses, the focus of John's interest fell, he can be fairly sure of the answer: on the work of Jesus Christ. . . . Whether we think of this document as a book, as a letter, or as a series of visions, Jesus Christ remains the central figure."[2]

The book of Revelation is about Jesus Christ. Period. End of discussion. With all the debates and confusion related to the interpretation of the book, there should be none on this point.[3] To understand the book of Revelation well it is essential to begin with John's description of Jesus.[4]

There is no question that for John, Jesus is the resurrected and glorified Lord of all creation. Thus, our first and primary key to learning how to interpret the book of Revelation properly is that the book is about Jesus.

---

1. Apocalypse is another name for the book of Revelation. The word derives from the Greek word *apokalypsis*, which is often translated "revelation."

2. Paul S. Minear, *I Saw a New Earth: An Introduction to the Visions of the Apocalypse* (Eugene, OR: Wipf & Stock, 2003), 11.

3. This is the great tragedy when it comes to the contemporary study of Revelation. Most Christians will not bother to even study the book—and understandably so. But then they miss out on the greatness of the book and its witness to the resurrected and glorified Jesus Christ. Others will attempt to study it, but often get so bogged down in discussions about tribulations, antichrists, and other such notions that they too miss out on the beauty of the study of Jesus Christ in the book.

4. That the author of the book of Revelation is named John can be seen in 1:9, where he names himself.

If our only objective were to read the book of Revelation to discern how Jesus is depicted, that would be a profitable exercise. Because Revelation presents us with the climax of the biblical story, and because this story focuses on Jesus, we neglect the study of this great work to our own peril. There is, however, further significance to John's portrayal of Jesus in the book of Revelation that cannot be overlooked, namely, that for John, Jesus is the model for the people of God to follow.

We will begin our focus in this chapter by investigating the significance of Jesus in the book of Revelation. Here we will examine the rich portrait of Jesus in its opening chapter. The For Further Study questions at the end of the chapter will allow the reader to discern John's depiction of Jesus in the remainder of Revelation.

THE BOOK IS ABOUT JESUS

To claim that the book of Revelation is about Jesus is easy to support. After all, the opening words of the book are "The Revelation of Jesus Christ" (1:1).

Although this phrase may appear straightforward and simplistic, its meaning is ambiguous—both in English and in the original Greek. This phrase can be understood to mean "The Revelation that is about Jesus Christ" or "The Revelation that is from Jesus Christ."[5]

When it comes to an ambiguity like this, the interpreter's best option is to read the text and see which meaning makes the most sense. Is it *about* Jesus or *from* Jesus? The difficulty is that after reading the book of Revelation one is still unsure which option best fits. This leads some to conclude, probably correctly, that John was intentionally unclear and that he wanted his readers to understand the book in light of both options: it is a revelation *about* Jesus Christ that is also *from* Jesus Christ.[6]

The great descriptions of Jesus in the book of Revelation highlight three principles: (1) Jesus is God made manifest and is worthy of the worship due to God alone. (2) Jesus is the fulfiller of God's promises in that He has

---

5. Although most English translations render this phrase as "The revelation of Jesus Christ," the NLT and NIV have chosen to eliminate any ambiguity by translating it: "The revelation from Jesus Christ." Of course, this translation assumes that this is what is meant. As we will see, the book could well be understood to be a "revelation about Jesus Christ."

6. This means that the translation "The revelation of Jesus Christ," though ambiguous itself, is likely the best.

accomplished the mission of God's people. (3) In fulfilling this mission, Jesus is the model for the people of God to emulate.

The last one is central for John. After all, John is not simply writing a theological treatise on the person and work of Christ. He is writing to the people of God. And He is not just telling us some great facts about Jesus. He is exhorting the churches to overcome as Jesus did.[7] Consequently, as we survey the book of Revelation to discern how Jesus is portrayed, it is important to note that the book of Revelation not only describes Christ in terms of His person—He is God made manifest and He is the resurrected and glorified Lord of all creation who is worthy of worship—but also as the One who has gone before us.

JESUS: THE FULFILLER OF THE MISSION OF GOD'S PEOPLE

In the book of Revelation Jesus is portrayed in terms of His work as the fulfiller of the mission of the people of God.[8] We will expand on this theme in chapter 2. For now, it is important to note that throughout the Scriptures the people of God are called to fulfill a mission. That mission is to make God known to the nations: "I will appoint you as a covenant to the people, as a light to the nations" (Isa. 42:6).[9] The book of Revelation highlights the fact that Jesus, as God among us, has faithfully accomplished this mission.[10]

---

7. We will look at this significant word "overcome" in some detail in chapter 3.

8. I find it easier and less confusing to use the designation "people of God" when referring to the chosen people—whether they are OT saints or NT saints. The problem is that using "Israel," which has several meanings, and "the church" often creates a disconnect for some readers. Since the book of Revelation traces a continuous line from Israel (i.e., the OT people of God), to Jesus, to the church (i.e., the NT people of God), it is easier and less confusing to refer to each as "the people of God." In doing so, it is anticipated that most readers will recognize the continuity between the two groups. See Kim Papaioannou, "'All Israel Will Be Saved': Establishing a Basis for a Valid Interpretation," *Ministry Journal* (November 2015): 6–9.

9. See also Isaiah 49:6.

10 This is an important point through the scope of the NT. In Luke 2 we see Simeon as he holds the Christ child declare, "For my eyes have seen Your salvation, which You have prepared in the presence of all peoples, A LIGHT OF REVELATION TO THE GENTILES" (Luke 2:30–32a). Note that the NASB places NT words or phrases in all caps when it wants to alert the reader that the word or phrase is a citation of the OT.

Now this does not mean that the mission has been completed and that there is no mission left for the people of God. On the contrary, Jesus has faithfully accomplished the mission and now He summons the people of God to carry it out to the nations.

JESUS: THE FAITHFUL WITNESS, THE FIRSTBORN FROM THE DEAD, THE RULER OF THE KINGS OF THE EARTH

In light of the fact that Jesus is depicted throughout Revelation as the resurrected, glorified, Lord of all creation, the opening description of Jesus comes somewhat as a surprise: "Jesus Christ, the faithful witness, the firstborn of the dead, and the ruler of the kings of the earth" (1:5).

There is something rather astonishing here, almost anti-climactic—if one can have a climax this early in the book. Throughout the book of Revelation, we see glorious descriptions and titles applied to Jesus: He is the One who is routinely worshiped by all who are before the throne of God (5:8). He is the One who is "the first and the last" (1:17; 2:8; 22:13). Yet despite all this, the first title ascribed to Jesus in the book of Revelation is the rather mundane "the faithful witness." This appears to be surprising. But once we begin to grasp John's larger purpose in the book of Revelation, we begin to realize that this is quite an appropriate opening description.

If John were merely writing a treatise on the person of Christ (which would be a worthy goal), we might have expected him to introduce Jesus by some other, loftier title. But if, as we will see throughout this book, John is also writing to exhort his churches to fulfill the mission of God's people to persevere in faithful witnessing as Christ has done, then it makes perfect sense why the first description of Jesus in the book of Revelation is that He is "the faithful witness."

In addition to this, Jesus is called "the firstborn of the dead and the ruler of the kings of the earth." Adding these two titles are meant to affirm that though Jesus' faithful witnessing led to His death, He is the One who defeated death and now reigns. In fact, one may well contend that the means by which Jesus became king was through His faithful witnessing, His suffering and death, and His resurrection.

Why, then, did John begin with these three titles? Because that is what we are to be also. Now, go follow the Lamb![11]

---

11. We will pick up this theme beginning in chapter 2.

We will continue to explore the significance of these titles over the next several chapters. The rest of this chapter will examine the opening description of Jesus in 1:12–20.

THE VISION OF JESUS CHRIST IN REVELATION 1:12–20

The primary vision of Jesus in Revelation 1 declares:

> In the middle of the lampstands I saw one like a son of man, clothed in a robe reaching to the feet, and girded across His chest with a golden sash. His head and His hair were white like white wool, like snow; and His eyes were like a flame of fire. His feet were like burnished bronze, when it has been made to glow in a furnace, and His voice was like the sound of many waters. In His right hand, He held seven stars, and out of His mouth came a sharp two-edged sword; and His face was like the sun shining in its strength. When I saw Him, I fell at His feet like a dead man. And He placed His right hand on me, saying, "Do not be afraid; I am the first and the last, and the living One; and I was dead, and behold, I am alive forevermore, and I have the keys of death and of Hades." (1:13–18)

In this opening vision, John sees the resurrected Christ. Jesus appears in all His unveiled glory! John begins by telling us that Jesus is wearing a "robe reaching to [His] feet" (1:13). Though this robe may in one sense portray Christ as both priest and king, the fact that John sees Jesus walking among the lampstands—which are themselves connected with the temple[12]—suggests that Jesus is more likely depicted here as the great priest.

Much of the description of Jesus in this vision is in language that is often applied to God. For example, John says that "His head and His hair were white like white wool, like snow" (1:14). This description echoes Daniel's vision of God Himself: "And the Ancient of Days took His seat; His vesture was like white snow and the hair of His head like pure wool" (Dan. 7:9).

---

12. Cf. Exodus 25:31–40; 27:20.

John also observes that Jesus' "eyes were like a flame of fire" (1:14). This corresponds to the numerous occasions in which God, as holy and judge, is associated with flaming fire.[13]

The description of Jesus' voice "like the sound of many waters" (1:15) parallels the portrayal of God in Ezekiel 43:2: "And behold, the glory of the God of Israel was coming from the way of the east. And His voice was like the sound of many waters; and the earth shone with His glory."

In addition, Jesus is also described in language corresponding to other essential attributes of God. The description of Jesus' feet "like burnished bronze" (1:15) suggests one who is morally pure. That Jesus has a "sharp two-edged sword" (1:16) coming from His mouth may well depict Him as the end-time judge. This is supported by the description of Jesus in Revelation 19. There John describes the returning Christ and indicates that

> from His mouth comes a sharp sword, so that with it He may strike down the nations. . . . And the rest were killed with the sword which came from the mouth of Him who sat on the horse (19:15, 21).

It is important to note that we must not think of Jesus as the end-time judge solely in relationship to His judgment on the nations. After all, that Jesus has a sword coming from His mouth serves as a strong warning to the church in Pergamum: "Therefore repent; or else I am coming to you quickly, and I will make war against them with the sword of My mouth" (2:16).

The final feature of John's description of Jesus in this opening vision is that "His face was like the sun" (1:16). Though there is a parallel with Matthew's description of Jesus at the transfiguration,[14] the language here accords more closely with the depiction of the victorious warrior in Judges 5 (cf. v. 31).[15] The link with Judges 5 may well serve to associate Jesus with

---

13. Cf. Exodus 3:2; Isaiah 30:30; 66:15; Daniel 7:9-12.

14. Matthew 17:2.

15. The link with Judges 5:31 is shown by the fact that the wording of Revelation 1:16 is in accordance with that of the Greek version of Judges 5:31. The connection is strengthened by the fact that the warrior of Judges 5 is linked with the "stars" (Judg. 5:20) just as Jesus holds the seven stars in His right hand. See Gregory K. Beale, *The Book of Revelation: A Commentary on the Greek Text* (Grand Rapids: Eerdmans, 1999), 212.

God as the divine warrior—a theme that is certainly present in the book of Revelation.[16]

John then tells us that Jesus placed His right hand upon him and exhorted him not to be afraid. After all, Jesus declares, "I am the first and the last" (1:17). This title further depicts Jesus as the eternal One. It is essentially the same title as applied to God the Father in 1:8.[17] The significance of this would have been unmistakable to a Jewish-Christian ear. After all, the designation "first and last" is applied to God in Isaiah 44:6: "Thus says the LORD, the King of Israel and his Redeemer, the LORD of hosts: 'I am the first and I am the last, and there is no God besides Me.'" This title explicitly indicates that God is the eternal One.

The opening vision of Jesus in the book of Revelation, then, emphatically declares that the One whom John has seen is Himself identified with the God of Israel.[18] It is also worth noting that the close of the book of Revelation reiterates this identification. In addition to being the "Alpha and the Omega" in 1:8, in 21:6 the Father Himself declares, "I am the Alpha and the Omega, the beginning and the end." Shortly thereafter, Jesus identifies Himself to John as "the Alpha and the Omega, the first and the last, the beginning and the end" (22:13).

In addition, Jesus further identifies Himself to John as "the living One; and I was dead, and behold, I am alive forevermore" (1:18). The importance here is not simply to declare that Jesus has risen from the dead, nor to identify Jesus as God, who is the living One,[19] but to encourage us that Jesus has risen from the dead and, therefore, so shall we. That is, because Jesus has risen from the dead, we have no reason to fear death. While it is true that "I was dead" (1:18), says Jesus, it is also true that "I am alive forevermore" (1:18).

---

16. We will look at the idea of holy war more fully in chapter 12.

17. Note that all three titles—"the Alpha and the Omega," "the first and the last," and "the beginning and the end"—are applied to Jesus in Revelation 22:13.

18. That Jesus is described in a manner that accords with the Father who sits on the throne in no way means that Jesus and the Father are the same in person. The book of Revelation clearly distinguishes between the Father who sits on the throne and the Lamb. For instance, in Revelation 5 the Father has a scroll in His hand that is then taken by the Lamb (5:7). The Lamb, Jesus, who takes the scroll, and the Father, from whom the scroll was taken, cannot be the same person.

19. Cf. Deuteronomy 32:40; Revelation 4:9.

Finally in 1:12–20, we learn that Jesus is not only alive but that He has "the keys of death and of Hades" (1:18). With this title, John encourages his readers, both then and now, with the realization that death has no power over the people of God. As Gordon Fee notes, "As a great preacher in the black tradition once told it on an Easter Sunday, playing the role of Satan, he shouted to the demonic host, 'He's got away! He's got away! And He's got the keys!'"[20]

For Further Study

1. Read and meditate on the descriptions of Jesus in the following passages and note the titles or attributes applied to Jesus: 1:5; 1:13; 1:17; 1:18; 2:1; 2:8; 2:12; 2:18; 3:1; 3:7; 3:14; 5:5; 5:6; 5:9; 5:12; 6:16; 11:15; 14:12; 15:3; 15:4; 17:14; 19:11; 22:13; 22:16; 22:20, 21. As you continue in this study, try to reflect on these descriptions and discern which ones might have been most significant to John and his readers and which titles or descriptions stand out to you.

2. Compare the use of the title "holy and true" in 3:7 and 6:10. To whom is it applied? What is the significance of this?

3. Compare the use of the titles "the First and the Last," "the Alpha and the Omega," and "the Beginning and the End" in 1:8, 17; 2:8; 21:6; 22:13. To whom are they applied? What does this mean for our understanding of Jesus and God the Father? (Note: compare this to Isa. 44:6 and 48:12).

4. What is the possible significance of the fact that Jesus is the "lamp" (21:23) and the seven churches are "lampstands" (1:20)?

5. Note the use of the titles "Lord (God) (Almighty)": 1:8; 4:8, 11; 11:15, 17; 15:3, 4; 16:7; 17:14; 18:8; 19:6, 16; 21:22; 22:6, 20, 21. To whom is it applied? Compare with Isaiah 45:5, 6, 18. What is the significance of this for Christian theology and worship?

6. Read the following passages and note the descriptions of praise that are given to the Father: 4:8; 5:13; 7:12; 19:1. Carefully compare this with the praise that is given to Jesus in 5:9, 12. How does this illuminate our understanding of Jesus in the book of Revelation?

7. In addition to 1:12–20, the other primary description of Jesus

---

20. Gordon Fee, *Revelation*, Kindle edition (Eugene, OR: Cascade Books, 2011), 19.

is 19:11–16. Note the differences between Jesus in 1:12–20 and 19:11–16. What might account for the differences? (Hint: try to determine the contextual differences between the two passages).

8. Compare the description of Jesus in 1:12–20 with the vision of the man in Daniel 10:5–6. What is the significance of this for our understanding of Revelation?

9. Note the titles and attributes of God the Father and Jesus that are applied, or appear to be applied, to others. What are the implications of this?

    a. Voice like the sound of many waters: 14:2.

    b. One like the son of man, having a gold crown on his head: 14:14.

    c. Seven angels who have golden girdles/sashes around their chests: 15:6.

Application

1. Discuss the importance of Revelation's portrayal of Jesus for Christian living.

2. As we will see in upcoming chapters, one of John's great concerns was to encourage his readers to persevere in faithful witnessing to the world. How does John's portrait of Jesus encourage us to be faithful witnesses? (Cite specific descriptions of Jesus in Revelation.)

CHAPTER 2

The People of God as Imitators of Christ

The book of Revelation is about Jesus, plain and simple. As I noted in chapter 1, He is the resurrected, glorified Lord of all creation, the "faithful witness," "the firstborn of the dead," and "the ruler of the kings of the earth" (1:5). The book of Revelation starts with and centers on the person of Jesus Christ. If we read Revelation only for its description of Jesus we would do well—but we would also be missing much.

The book of Revelation may also be viewed as a manifesto, a call to the people of God. Sure, John wrote about Jesus. He did so, however, not simply that we might know Christ and who He is. Rather, he wrote to exhort the people of God to faithfully imitate Christ and fulfill God's mission to the nations. This is the significance of the fact that Jesus is the lamp (21:23) and the people of God are the lampstands (1:20): the people of God make known the light by imitating Jesus.[1] This is likely the reason why, of all the glorious descriptions of Jesus in Revelation, the first title ascribed to Him is "the faithful witness" (1:5). As stated in the previous chapter, this might appear odd: Why would John give us this rather mundane title as his first description of Christ? The answer is that Jesus is the model that the people of God are to imitate. John begins with Jesus as the "faithful witness" because this is the very thing that the people of God are called to be.

---

1. In the For Further Study section we will look more carefully at John's use of "lamp" in the book of Revelation.

Herein lies another reason why it is so vital to discern John's portrait of Jesus. Without a proper understanding of Christ, we cannot completely discern John's message to the churches regarding their mission. As C. B. Caird has noted, "Each Christian is called to an *imitatio Christi*, a holding fast to the testimony of Jesus. Each is called to be a Conqueror, repeating in his own life the archetypal victory of Christ."[2]

FULFILLING GOD'S MISSION: THE PEOPLE OF GOD AND THE SEVEN LAMPSTANDS

The vision in Revelation chapter 1 begins with John seeing "one like a son of man" standing amidst seven lampstands (1:12–20). John is told that the lampstands represent the seven churches of Asia (1:20).[3] Though John is not offered any explanation as to what significance there might be to the lampstands, it would seem that one was not needed. The book of Revelation's use of lampstands as symbols of the seven churches surely conveyed that the primary mission of the churches was to display the light.

What is important here is that we are to read this not only as a statement of what the people of God are but also of what the people of God are to do. That is, Jesus was not merely bestowing on His disciples a status. He was also giving them a mission. The designation "lampstands," then, is not just an honorific title. This designation meant that the churches were called to make known the light to the nations.[4]

In order to affirm the thesis that the people of God are called to imitate Christ, specifically in terms of the missional call of making God known, we will need to briefly digress from our look at the book of Revelation and bring into focus the scope of the biblical witness.

The OT People of God Are to Be the Light of the World

Throughout the OT, we see that the people of God were chosen for a purpose. The clearest indication is found in the book of Isaiah: "I will also

---

2. George Bradford Caird, *A Commentary on the Revelation of St. John the Divine* (New York: Harper, 1966), 297.

3. Asia was a province in the Roman Empire in what is today western Turkey.

4. One of the problems in contemporary Christianity is that many Christians conceive of salvation or chosenness as something that exclusively benefits the recipient: "I am chosen and therefore I get to go to heaven—it is for me." But in Scripture being chosen is for a purpose. See especially 1 Peter 2:9–10 cited below.

make you a light of the nations so that My salvation may reach to the end of the earth" (Isa. 49:6; cf. Isa. 42:6). Isaiah makes it clear that the people of God were set apart in order to make God known to the nations.

Jesus Is the Light of the World

It is in this context that we are to understand Jesus' declaration that He is "the light of the world" (John 8:12; 9:5). What Isaiah longed for finds its fulfillment in Jesus—He is the One through whom God will be made known to the nations. What the people of God were called to do, Jesus did. He was faithful as the light of the world. The very same mission that the OT people of God were called to fulfill is the mission that Jesus fulfilled.

This is evident in the proclamation of Simeon in the Gospel of Luke. Luke tells us the story of a righteous old man named Simeon who was promised that he would see the Christ before he died (Luke 2:25–26). When the baby Jesus arrived in the temple, Simeon affirms, "My eyes have seen Your salvation, which You have prepared in the presence of all peoples, A LIGHT OF REVELATION TO THE GENTILES, and the glory of Your people Israel" (Luke 2:30–32). Simeon, citing Isaiah 42:6 and 49:6, declares that Jesus is the fulfillment of the mission of God's people. What God had called the people of God to do was accomplished by Jesus.

This is straightforward enough and many Christians have this basic understanding of the role of Jesus. The NT, however, does not stop here.

The NT People of God Are to Be the Light of the World

I have already noted that the NT people of God are expressly referred to as "the light of the world" (Matt. 5:14). What is important to understand is that the task of being the light of the world is also in accord with the mission for the OT people of God.

The book of Acts records the efforts of Paul and Barnabas to carry out God's mission to the Roman world. In Acts 13 we learn that Paul and Barnabas had been proclaiming the gospel among the local Jewish community in Pisidian Antioch. Finally, after several weeks of preaching, they were run out of the synagogue. Upon their expulsion, Paul proclaims to the Jewish leadership that they will leave and focus their preaching on the Gentile (non-Jewish) communities. Paul explains that the reason why this must happen is because "the Lord has commanded us, 'I HAVE PLACED

YOU AS A LIGHT FOR THE GENTILES, THAT YOU MAY BRING
SALVATION TO THE END OF THE EARTH'" (Acts 13:47). As the
all caps in the NASB indicates Paul is citing Scripture to explain why he
and Barnabas must leave the Jewish community and turn to the nations.
The Scripture that he cites is Isaiah 49:6. This means that Paul has cited,
and applied to himself and Barnabas, the very same Scripture that Simeon
cited and applied to Jesus.

At first glance we might wonder how this can be. After all, were not the
Isaiah passages fulfilled by Jesus? And if these passages were fulfilled by
Jesus, how can they also be applied to Paul and Barnabas?

The answer is that the same mission that God gave to the OT people of
God was the mission that Jesus fulfilled. It was also the mission that Paul
and Barnabas carried out. And it is the mission that all of God's people are
called to carry out. The fulfillment of the mission was begun by Jesus; the
completion of the mission is the task of the people of God.

This is why Jesus can declare that He Himself is the light of the world
(John 8:12; 9:5). And yet He can also declare that His disciples are the
light of the world (Matt. 5:14).[5]

The notion that the people of God are called, or chosen, for a purpose is
very clear in Peter's affirmation:

> But you are A CHOSEN RACE, A royal PRIESTHOOD, A
> HOLY NATION, A PEOPLE FOR God's OWN POSSESSION,
> so that you may proclaim the excellencies of Him who has called
> you out of darkness into His marvelous light. (1 Peter 2:9)

What is essential in 1 Peter 2:9 is the "so that."[6] The conjunction (*hopos*)
behind the text of 1 Peter expresses purpose. In other words, 1 Peter 2:9
may well be translated as "you were chosen *for the purpose of* proclaiming."
Note also that 1 Peter associates the missional calling of the people of God
with the imagery of light: "so that you may proclaim the excellencies of
Him who has called you out of darkness into His marvelous light" (1 Peter
2:9).

---

5. See also Philippians 2:15.

6. NASB. The NLT says "as a result"; the NRSV says "in order that"; the ESV, NIV,
and NET say "that."

It is here that this all becomes important for our study of the book of Revelation. I have already noted that it was very likely that the seven churches to whom John was writing knew well that the OT people of God were called to be a light to the nations. They also knew that Jesus, Paul and Barnabas, and even they themselves were called to carry out this mission. Thus, the seven churches could be symbolized as lampstands and no explanation would have been necessary.

THE PEOPLE OF GOD ARE TO EMULATE JESUS

As we have already observed, John opens the book of Revelation by ascribing to Jesus the three titles of "faithful witness," "firstborn from the dead," and "ruler of the kings of the earth" (1:5). These titles serve to provide more than just a description of Jesus.

Now we see that Jesus is the One whom the people of God are to emulate. The fact that "the faithful witness" is the first description of Jesus in the book of Revelation is significant—John wants to encourage his readers that just as Jesus was the faithful witness so shall they be also.

The other two titles in Revelation 1:5 are also important. They serve to further enhance John's overall focus on following the Lamb. Thus, Jesus is "the firstborn from the dead." This title is intended to provide confidence for the people of God—even if you are killed, you too will be resurrected. After all, if Jesus is the firstborn, then you shall be second!

The third title, "the ruler of the kings of the earth," also serves to reinforce John's exhortation to the people of God. Since Jesus is the ruler of the kings of the earth, we are to be encouraged by the reminder that He is the world's true Lord. It is in light of this that we recognize the importance of the fact that the people of God are themselves "a kingdom, priests to His God and Father" (1:6).

That the people of God are to emulate Jesus, then, provides the key to understanding the significance of the great affirmation that the people of God "are the ones who follow the Lamb wherever He goes" (14:4).

Herein lies the significance for understanding one of the great promises in the book of Revelation: "He who overcomes, I will grant to him to sit down with Me on My throne, as I also overcame and sat down with My Father on His throne" (3:21). The repeated exhortation to overcome, which we will examine in the next chapter, is the primary appeal to the people of God in the book of Revelation. Notice, however, that in Revelation 3:21

our overcoming is directly associated with Christ's overcoming: "He who overcomes . . . as I also overcame."

CONCLUSION

We might say, then, that the book was written first to depict Christ and His finished work. To this we must add that it was also written as a manifesto to the people of God in order that they might act. These two things, of course, must not be separated. The book of Revelation sets the work of God's people in the context of carrying out the mission of Christ in imitation of Christ. The descriptions of Jesus in the book of Revelation serve to remind us of who He is, what He has done, and what we are called to do: Follow the Lamb!

For Further Study

1. Now that we have learned that Jesus is the model for the people of God to emulate, re-examine some of the key titles for Jesus from the previous chapter and ask what the significance of these titles are for the people of God today. Some examples include:
   a. Jesus is "Faithful and True" (3:14; 19:11). Compare with the exhortation to the people of God to be "faithful" (2:10) and the description of those with Christ who are the "called and chosen and faithful" (17:14).
   b. Jesus is "the firstborn of the dead" (1:5). Compare with those who "came to life" (20:4).
2. As mentioned in the previous chapter, the first title given to Jesus is that He is the "faithful witness" (1:5; cf. 3:14). What is the significance of the fact that Antipas is called "My witness, My faithful one" (2:13)?[7]
3. One of the descriptions of Jesus in the opening vision is that "His voice was like the sound of many waters" (1:15). Note the use of the sound/voice of "many waters" in 14:2 and 19:6. What might this

---

7. The translation here does not associate the two verses as much as the Greek text does. The Greek of Revelation 1:5 and 2:13 is virtually the same. Both verses have "the witness, the faithful." The only difference is that in 2:13 Jesus is speaking and He calls Antipas "my," so that 2:13 in the Greek reads "the witness my, the faithful my," which is translated as "my faithful witness" in the ESV, NET, NIV, and NLT.

mean for our understanding of the book of Revelation?

4. There are a few occasions in Revelation where it is difficult to determine if an individual is an angel, a mere human being, or Christ Himself.

   a. Compare the "strong angel" of 10:1–3 and the description of Christ in 1:12–20 and 5:5–7. Is this an angel or Jesus?

   b. Compare 14:14 where we see "one like a son of man" sitting on a cloud. Is this Christ or an angel?[8]

   c. Discuss how this might help account for why, on two occasions, John attempts to worship the one who is speaking with him only to be rebuked (19:10; 22:8–9).

5. The two witnesses in Revelation 11 are said to be killed and "their dead bodies will lie in the street of the great city which mystically is called Sodom and Egypt, where also their Lord was crucified" (11:8). What is the significance of the fact that they are killed in the same place as where "their Lord was crucified"?[9] Does this help us identify what this city/place this might be, or does John note this for some other reason?

6. What other parallels are there between Jesus and the description of the two witnesses?

Application

1. In view of what we have learned in chapters 1 and 2 of this study, why is it important to study Jesus and the people of God in the book of Revelation?[10]

---

8. Part of the difficulty here is due to the nature of apocalyptic language, a subject I will discuss in chapter 6.

9. It is not important at this juncture to try to identify the two witnesses. Resist the urge to do so.

10. Note that all the books of the Bible were written in large measure to people in order to influence the beliefs and practices of the people of God.

CHAPTER 3

"Overcome": Revelation's Most Important Word

W e have seen that the book of Revelation is about Jesus and that it exhorts the people of God to imitate Christ in faithful witnessing. Now we turn to the most important word in the book of Revelation, the Greek verb *nikaō*. Unpacking *nikaō* (which is commonly translated "overcome" or "conquer") will greatly enhance our ability to interpret the book of Revelation.

NIKAŌ: OVERCOME/CONQUER

The word *nikaō* occurs twenty-eight times in the NT,[1] seventeen of which are found in the book of Revelation. The word is variously translated in our English Bibles.[2] Its primary meanings are "overcome," "conquer," and "be the victor." The word "overcome" appears for the first time in the book of Revelation in the seven letters of chapters 2

---

1. Luke 11:22; John 16:33; Romans 3:4; 12:21 (twice); 1 John 2:13, 14; 4:4; 5:4 (twice); 5:5; Revelation 2:7, 11, 17, 26; 3:5, 12, 21 (twice); 5:5; 6:2 (twice); 11:7; 12:11; 13:7; 15:2; 17:14; 21:7.

2. The NASB translates it with some form of "overcome" throughout Revelation with only the following exceptions: "conquering" and "to conquer" (6:2); and "victorious" (15:2). The NIV translates *nikaō* as "overcome" less consistently: exceptions include "triumphed" (5:5); "conqueror" and "bent on conquest" (6:2); "overpower" (11:7); "to conquer" (13:7); "victorious" (15:2); and "triumph" (17:14). The ESV is the most consistent. It uses some form of the word "conquer" throughout the book of Revelation.

and 3.[3] In fact, each of the seven letters concludes with an exhortation for the churches to overcome.

To the church in Ephesus: "To him who overcomes, I will grant to eat of the tree of life, which is in the Paradise of God" (2:7). To the church in Smyrna: "He who overcomes shall not be hurt by the second death" (2:11). To the church in Pergamum: "To him who overcomes, to him I will give some of the hidden manna, and I will give him a white stone, and a new name written on the stone which no one knows but he who receives it" (2:17). To the church in Thyatira: "He who overcomes, and he who keeps My deeds until the end, TO HIM I WILL GIVE AUTHORITY OVER THE NATIONS; AND HE SHALL RULE THEM WITH A ROD OF IRON, AS THE VESSELS OF THE POTTER ARE BROKEN TO PIECES, as I also have received authority from My Father; and I will give him the morning star" (2:26–28). To the church in Sardis: "He who overcomes shall thus be clothed in white garments; and I will not erase his name from the book of life, and I will confess his name before My Father, and before His angels" (3:5). To the church in Philadelphia: "He who overcomes, I will make him a pillar in the temple of My God, and he will not go out from it anymore; and I will write upon him the name of My God, and the name of the city of My God, the new Jerusalem, which comes down out of heaven from My God, and My new name" (3:12). And to the church in Laodicea: "He who overcomes, I will grant to him to sit down with Me on My throne, as I also overcame and sat down with My Father on His throne" (3:21).

It is evident from this that the exhortation to overcome forms one of the central appeals in the book of Revelation. No church is exempt; they are all exhorted to overcome. It is important to recognize that most of John's audience would have *heard* the book read to them. One person would read the scroll, while the rest listened. Because they were accustomed to listening to such texts, the hearers would have been prepared to recognize repetitions as a means of stressing what is important. This means that the repeated use of overcome at the end of each of the seven letters would not have been missed by John's hearers.

---

3. Revelation 1:4 tells us that the book is addressed to seven of the churches of Asia. Each of the seven churches is briefly addressed in the form of these seven letters in Revelation 2 and 3.

The application of the message of Revelation for us today follows very easily here. Regardless of what one's view of the seven churches might be,[4] we can easily conclude that since John exhorts all the churches to overcome, he surely wants us to do the same. This raises the important question: What does it mean to overcome?

OVERCOMING AND FAITHFUL WITNESSING

The presence of this exhortation in each of the seven letters is significant. I have already noted that the seven churches are symbolized by lampstands, and that this imagery conveys to us that the very nature of the churches was such that they were to serve as God's witnesses. The question becomes how closely we should connect the exhortation to overcome with the churches' role as witnesses. Could it be that John was implying that their witnessing activity would result in the need to overcome? That is, would their witnessing result in hardships, suffering, persecution, and even death?

The best way to discern this, of course, is to continue reading. As we proceed through the book of Revelation it indeed appears that the suffering of the people of God is directly connected with their witness. The people of God are called to be God's spokespersons for the world. But no one said it would be easy.[5]

OVERCOMING MODELED ON CHRIST'S OVERCOMING

The letter to the church in Laodicea is the seventh and final letter in Revelation chapters 2-3. The very nature of the fact that it is the final letter provides it with a natural prominence. Furthermore, that the word "overcome" occurs twice in this letter adds to its significance. John writes,

---

4. There are a variety of views regarding the seven churches. Virtually all recognize them as seven historical churches that existed at the time of John's writings. Others consider them to also be representative of seven epochs of church history. Those who suggest this usually propose that we are in the seventh epoch of Laodicea today. Beyond recognizing that they were seven historical churches to whom John wrote this book, identifying them further is not necessary for the purposes of our study.

5. The importance of this point for Christian living cannot be overestimated. Reading and understanding the book of Revelation well causes us to soon realize that the Christian life is not a game. It is not something to be taken lightly. And it is not something that we can be passive participants in. As we will see later in this book, the dragon is at war with God's people; therefore, overcoming is necessary and something to be taken seriously.

"He who overcomes . . . as I also overcame" (3:21). Note, also, that the overcoming of the people of God is directly connected with Christ's overcoming. That is, just as the people of God were to be faithful witnesses in imitation of Christ, so also they are to overcome just as He did.

In order to appreciate the full force of this exhortation, however, we must discern more precisely what it means to overcome as Jesus did in the book of Revelation.

JESUS' OVERCOMING

One of the most significant uses of overcome in the book of Revelation occurs in the description of the Lion and the Lamb in Revelation 5. The chapter opens with John seeing a scroll that is sealed up with seven seals in the right hand of the Father (5:1). We then learn that John looks for someone who can open the scroll, but he finds no one who is "able to open the book, or to look into it" (5:3). Then he begins to weep (5:4). An angel then admonishes him to stop weeping because "the Lion that is from the tribe of Judah, the Root of David, has overcome so as to open the book and its seven seals" (5:5). Immediately, John turns to look: "And I saw between the throne (with the four living creatures) and the elders a Lamb standing, as if slain" (5:6). These verses bring us to the heart of the message of the book of Revelation.

First, we observe that John *hears* that "the Lion . . . has overcome" (5:5). But when John turns to look, presumably to see the lion, he instead *sees* "a Lamb standing, as if slain" (5:6). It would be understandable if our initial reaction might be to assume that John heard one thing (that a lion has overcome) but saw something else (a lamb that was slain). Many students of the Bible, however, will recognize immediately that both the images of a lion and of a lamb reflect the person and work of Christ—Jesus is the Lion *and* the Lamb. John does not hear one thing and see another—both images are of Christ.

In Scripture, the imagery of a lion occurs as an expression of kingship. Genesis 49:9–10a notes,

> Judah is a lion's whelp;
> From the prey, my son, you have gone up.
> He couches, he lies down as a lion,
> And as a lion, who dares rouse him up?

> The scepter shall not depart from Judah,
> Nor the ruler's staff from between his feet

Here we see that the kingly lineage in Israel was to descend from the tribe of Judah. Jesus, of course, was a descendant of Judah (cf. Matt. 1:2–3; Heb. 7:14), and He is thereby qualified to be the king. Jesus, then, is the Lion.

Yet Jesus is also the Lamb. The use of lamb imagery in Scripture is commonly associated with the sacrificial Passover lamb. We see this in the Gospel of John when John the Baptist declares to his followers that Jesus is "the Lamb of God who takes away the sin of the world" (John 1:29, 36).

The most significant association of Jesus with the lamb is found in connection with his fulfillment of the great Isaianic prophecy of the suffering servant (Isa. 52:13–53:12). The suffering servant is described by Isaiah as a lamb: "Like a lamb that is led to slaughter, and like a sheep that is silent before its shearers, so He did not open His mouth" (Isa. 53:7).

That Jesus is the fulfillment of the slain lamb in Isaiah 53 is abundantly clear in the NT. The Gospel of Matthew, for example, quotes Isaiah 53:4 and applies it to Jesus:

> When evening came, they brought to Him many who were demon-possessed; and He cast out the spirits with a word, and healed all who were ill. This was to fulfill what was spoken through Isaiah the prophet: "HE HIMSELF TOOK OUR INFIRMITIES AND CARRIED AWAY OUR DISEASES." (Matt. 8:16–17)

In addition, the book of Acts narrates an encounter between Philip and an Ethiopian. The Ethiopian was reading Isaiah 53:7–8 and then asks Philip "Please tell me, of whom does the prophet say this? Of himself or of someone else?" (Acts 8:34). Luke, the author of Acts, then explains that "then Philip opened his mouth, and beginning from this Scripture he preached Jesus to him" (Acts 8:35).

Additional references to Jesus as the fulfillment of the suffering lamb of Isaiah are found throughout the NT. First Peter 2:22 applies Isaiah 53:9 to Jesus. In the Gospel of Luke, Jesus Himself cites Isaiah 53:12 and claims to be the fulfillment: "For I tell you that this which is written must be fulfilled in Me, 'AND HE WAS NUMBERED WITH TRANSGRESSORS'; for that which refers to Me has its fulfillment" (Luke 22:37). In addition, Matthew 27:12–14 accounts for Jesus' silence at His trial as an echo of Isaiah 53:7. Finally, the Gospel of John notes that the rejection of Jesus by many is accounted for in the prophecy of Isaiah:

> But though He had performed so many signs before them, yet they were not believing in Him. This was to fulfill the word of Isaiah the prophet which he spoke: "LORD, WHO HAS BELIEVED OUR REPORT? AND TO WHOM HAS THE ARM OF THE LORD BEEN REVEALED?" (John 12:37–38; cf. Isa. 53:1)

OVERCOMING AND SUFFERING:
THE IRONIC NOTION OF OVERCOMING

What is the significance of all this? Quite simply, there is an ironic sense to the meaning of overcome in the book of Revelation: *Jesus is the Lion who rules as king because He was the Lamb who was slain.* That is, the means through which Jesus has overcome, so as to be the ruling Lion, was by His being the Lamb that was slain! This is the significance of John's *hearing* that the Lion has overcome, but afterwards looking and *seeing* a Lamb who was slain.

Throughout the book of Revelation, in fact, Jesus' kingly rule is closely tied to His sacrificial surrendering of His life as the Lamb of God. Thus, in Revelation 17:14, Jesus' kingship is directly tied with His being the Lamb: "These will wage war against the Lamb, and the Lamb will overcome them, because He is Lord of lords and King of kings, and those who are with Him are the called and chosen and faithful."

THE PEOPLE OF GOD AND THE
IRONIC NOTION OF OVERCOMING

To fully comprehend the command to overcome in the book of Revelation we must grasp the centrality of the ironic notion of overcoming. In the book of Revelation, the people of God are to overcome as Jesus did. In doing so, we too will become kings and queens, sitting with Him on His throne (3:21). Now we realize that Jesus has overcome and become the King by means of being the Lamb who was slain.

CONCLUSION

This is the heart of the message of the book of Revelation. The book of Revelation is about Jesus. An important aspect of John's depiction of Jesus is that He is the model that the people of God are to emulate. We are to "follow the Lamb" wherever He goes. Since Jesus is the "faithful witness" (1:5), then so shall we be. And we are to faithfully live out and proclaim the gospel to the end just as Jesus did. This is what it means to "overcome . . . as I also overcame" (3:21).

Observe the ironic notion of overcoming in the description of the people of God in Revelation 12:11: "And they overcame him because of the blood of the Lamb and because of the word of their testimony, and they did not love their life even when faced with death." Whoever John is describing in Revelation 12, beyond the fact that they are followers of Christ, is not of concern to us at this juncture of our study. What is essential for interpreting the book of Revelation is that those who overcome are the ones who willingly laid down their lives.

Up to this point in our study we have learned that the book of Revelation is about Jesus. It is not, however, merely a theological guide to knowing and understanding Jesus. Instead, we see that John is deeply concerned that his readers know and understand Jesus so that they might follow the Lamb.

Now we have begun to discern what following the Lamb means. Its meaning corresponds with the words of Jesus in the Gospels: "If anyone wishes to come after Me, he must deny himself, and take up his cross and follow Me" (Mark 8:34). Jesus was faithful to the end. And the people of God are called to do the same.

Though we have a long way to go in our understanding of the book of Revelation, it is important to note at this point that we can affirm that Revelation is deeply concerned with the present. The people of God have a mission to carry out. Their mission is to follow the Lamb wherever He goes. To do so, they will have to overcome.

For Further Study

1. Examine each occurrence of *nikaō* ("overcome") in the book of Revelation and describe what overcoming looks like. That is, who or what is overcome? How are they to overcome? (2:7, 11, 17, 26; 3:5, 12, 21; 5:5; 6:2; 11:7; 12:11; 13:7; 15:2; 17:14; 21:7).

2. Examine the use of *nikaō* in the Gospel of John and the letters of John (John 16:33; 1 John 2:13, 14; 4:4; 5:4, 5). How does this help us understand the use of *nikaō* in the book of Revelation?

3. After examining the use of *nikaō* in the book of Revelation listed above, what do you think was one of John's primary motivations in writing the book?

4. In addition to the exhortation to overcome, John also uses the word *hypomonē,* "persevere" (also translated "endurance" [NET]; "patient endurance" [ESV, NIV, NLT]; "patience" [NKJV]). In fact, John's opening description of himself, is "your brother and fellow partaker in the tribulation, kingdom, and perseverance" (1:9). Examine John's use of *hypomonē* in the book of Revelation and note how this might add to our understanding of John's purpose for writing this book (1:9; 2:2, 3, 19; 3:10; 13:10; 14:12).

5. Observe John's reference to tribulation (1:9; 2:9, 10, 22; 7:14). According to these verses, who are the ones who are enduring the tribulation? (Note that it might be essential here to rid oneself of any popular notions of tribulation. At this point, only allow the word to be defined by the text of Revelation).

6. Examine the presence of the expression "I am coming" in 2:5, 16; 3:11; 16:15; 22:7, 12, 20. Note that each occurrence is directed to the people of God. How does this help us discern John's purpose for writing?

7. Observe that five of the seven letters to the churches contain the exhortation "I know your deeds/works" (2:2, 19; 3:1, 8, 15). Examine 9:20 and 16:11 and note that many did not repent of their deeds/works and the consequences that are given in 18:6; 20:12–13. Then examine the final exhortation given by Christ in 22:12. What is the possible significance of this?

8. As we proceed in our study it will be essential to discern not only what it means to overcome but what it is that we are to overcome. Read through Revelation 17–18 and begin to ask who or what the harlot might be and what it means for the church today. (Note that one may want to skip ahead and read chapter 10 on dualism).

Application

1. What might it mean to overcome today? Note that one of the great dangers to the church is to assume that because many of us do not face persecution or any overt opposition to our Christian beliefs and practices we have no need to overcome. What do you think John would have to say about this?
2. Think of Christians in other parts of the world. What might overcoming look like for them? How might we help the church around the world overcome?
3. What are some important steps we might take to be more prepared to overcome?

CHAPTER 4

Imagery and the Old Testament

This final chapter in the first part of our study presents us with a second key to reading the book of Revelation in the twenty-first century. This second key is that the imagery in Revelation comes primarily from the OT. The imagery of lions and sheep, women clothed with the sun, harlots, the sun being darkened, water being turned into blood, men hiding in caves, scrolls that are eaten, people that are sealed, lambs that are slain, beasts, dragons, and more—all have their primary roots in the OT. John was not seeing the future per se. He was seeing Jesus. He was seeing Jesus, however, in light of His fulfillment of the OT.

In order to determine the meaning of the imagery in the book of Revelation it is important to discern what the images and symbols meant in their original OT context. From there we can determine how John may have understood them in light of Jesus.

This chapter will briefly survey some of the most important OT backgrounds for the images in the book of Revelation. I will then address their significance for our understanding of Revelation.

THE LIKELY OLD TESTAMENT BACKGROUNDS
FOR SOME OF THE IMAGES IN REVELATION

We will begin our survey in Revelation 4.[1] Revelation chapters 4 and 5 open the visionary section of Revelation with a description of God on His

---

1. I have already noted that the opening description of Jesus in Revelation 1 draws heavily on the depictions of God in the OT and that this description of Jesus is central to the seven letters of chapters 2 and 3.

throne. The description of One sitting on a throne in Revelation 4–5 derives largely from Daniel 7:6–27. In fact, there are fourteen items in Revelation 4–5 that are found in Daniel 7 in virtually the same order.[2] In addition, there are also parallels to the vision of God in Ezekiel chapters 1–2.[3]

The imagery in these chapters also draws upon several other OT passages. The seven lamps that were burning before the throne in Revelation 4:5 remind the reader of the seven lamps in Zechariah 4:2–10. The four living creatures in Revelation 4:6–8 parallel the cherubim in Ezekiel 1:5–21 and possibly the seraphim of Isaiah 6:2–3. The scroll of 5:1, which is in the right hand of the Father (which may be the same scroll that John is told to eat in Revelation 10:9–10), recalls the scroll in Ezekiel, which Ezekiel is also told to eat (Ezek. 2:8–3:3).

The primary background for the vision of the breaking of the seven seals beginning in Revelation 6 is both Ezekiel 14:12–13 and Zechariah 6:1–8. The first four seals appear as trials that confront believers. This is made explicit in the fifth seal, where the souls of the righteous are crying out for vindication (6:9–11).[4] Interestingly, the greatest parallel for the seals occurs in Jesus' Olivet Discourse (Matt. 24:4–13; Mark 13:5–25; Luke 21:8–12). Of course, the Olivet Discourse itself draws heavily upon the OT for its imagery.

In Revelation 7 the imagery of the sealing of the 144,000 from each of the tribes of Israel has as its primary background Ezekiel 9:3–10. In addition, the counting of the twelve tribes in Revelation 7:4–8 coincides with the numbering of the Israelites in preparation for war in the book of Numbers (Num. 1:3, 18, 20; 26:1–65).

The description of the seven trumpets in Revelation 8–9 uses an array of images from throughout the OT.[5] The theme of the exodus, which is significant for much of the imagery in the book of Revelation, is especially prominent among the seven trumpets.[6]

---

2. Gregory K. Beale, *The Book of Revelation: A Commentary on the Greek Text* (Grand Rapids: Eerdmans, 1999), 415.

3. Some of the significance of this background for our understanding of the book of Revelation is found in John's development of the Trinity—for the worship of God in these OT passages is then transferred to Christ also in the book of Revelation.

4. See chapter 9 for further discussion of the souls under the altar.

5. The seven trumpets actually continue into Revelation 11 (note 11:15).

6. Of the seven trumpets, it is the first five that are patterned on the exodus. Compare Revelation 8:7 with Exodus 9:22–25; Revelation 8:8–11 with Exodus 7:20–25; Revelation 8:12 with Exodus 10:21–23; and Revelation 9:1–11 with Exodus 10:12–15.

In Revelation 10 we see an angel with a scroll in his right hand, which is similar to the one in the Father's hand (cf. 5:1). John is instructed, just as Ezekiel was (Ezek. 2:8–3:3), to eat the scroll (10:9–10). This OT background is important in that the Ezekiel text is the prophetic commissioning of Ezekiel. After Ezekiel eats the scroll, he is commissioned: "Son of man, go to the house of Israel and speak with My words to them" (Ezek. 3:4). In a similar manner John is commissioned as a prophet. He too, after eating the scroll, is told, "You must prophesy again concerning many peoples and nations and tongues and kings" (10:11).

Revelation 11 begins with John measuring a temple (11:1–2). The most prominent background for the temple imagery throughout Revelation is the great temple description in Ezekiel 40–48.[7]

Revelation 11 then narrates the story of the two witnesses. Among the many OT sources for these two prophets are the stories of Moses and Elijah. For just as Moses turned the waters into blood (Exod. 7:14–25), and Elijah shut up the sky so that rain did not fall (1 Kings 17:1), so also the two witnesses have the same abilities (11:6). In addition, the fact that there are *two* witnesses derives from the OT provision that two or three witnesses were required to validate a testimony (cf. Deut. 17:6).[8] Finally, the lampstands and the olive trees of Zechariah 4:2–14 provide the background for the following description of the two witnesses: "These are the two olive trees and the two lampstands that stand before the Lord of the earth" (11:4).

Revelation chapter 12 carries forward the narrative of the book of Revelation by presenting the story of a woman who was with child and being pursued by a dragon. This woman is described as being "clothed with the sun, and the moon under her feet, and on her head a crown of twelve stars" (12:1). The likely background for the vision of the woman (12:1–2) is

---

7. The temple-city of Ezekiel 40–48 is very significant throughout the NT in general and the book of Revelation in particular. This passage lies prominently behind the description of the temple-city in Revelation 19–22, as will be mentioned below. There are many passages in Scripture that could be brought forth as central to John's depiction of the temple in the book of Revelation, including many NT examples, which themselves are based on OT precursors (e.g., 1 Cor. 3:16–17; 6:19; 2 Cor. 6:16; Eph. 2:21–22; 1 Peter 2:5).

8. This is also the likely context for understanding Jesus' sending of the twelve and the seventy in pairs.

the dream of Joseph in Genesis 37:9. In Genesis 37, Joseph has a dream in which the sun, moon, and eleven stars were bowing down to him.

Revelation 13 presents us with the accounts of two beasts. Whoever or whatever they are, we know this: they are bad. The first beast blasphemes God Himself (13:6) and makes war against God's people (13:7). The second deceives the world (13:14) so that the people of the world ally with the first beast in opposition to God's people. The definitive background for the first beast (13:1–8) is Daniel 7.[9] When one compares the four beasts of Daniel 7 to the first beast in Revelation 13, the parallels are striking. There is, however, a key difference between the beasts of Daniel 7 and the first beast of Revelation 13. Most notably, the first beast in Revelation 13 appears to be a composite of all four of the beasts in Daniel 7. Daniel's four beasts have a total of seven heads (Dan. 7:4–7), while in Revelation 13 the first beast has seven heads (13:1). The fourth beast in Daniel has ten horns (Dan. 7:7) just as this first beast in Revelation (13:1). The result is that Revelation 13:1–8 appears to have combined the four beasts of Daniel 7 into one.

The description of the second beast in Revelation 13:11–18 is not as rich in the imagery of the OT as the first beast. This is due in part to the fact that this beast is described more in terms of its role of causing everyone to worship the first beast. The most prominent OT sources for this beast are in Ezekiel 9.

As we continue through the book of Revelation, we begin to notice that many of the same images recur.[10] The 144,000, for instance, reappear in Revelation 14:1–5, where they are seen standing with Christ on Mount Zion.

Revelation 14 also presents us with three angels who proclaim the coming of the hour of judgment (14:7). The OT parallels for the events following this proclamation include Psalms 96–100, Daniel 4:30, and Isaiah 51:17. Revelation 14 closes with references to two harvests. The first is the harvest of grain (14:14–16) and the second is the harvest of grapes (14:17–20). Though the primary text behind the two harvests is Isaiah 63:1–6, the notion of the harvest is abundant in the OT.

---

9. Cf. Revelation 13:1 to Daniel 7:2–3, 7; Revelation 13:2 to Daniel 7:3–6; Revelation 13:4 to Daniel 7:6, 12; Daniel 13:5 to Daniel 7:8, 25; Revelation 13:6 to Daniel 7:25; and Revelation 13:7 to Daniel 7:14, 21.

10. The importance of this will be discussed in chapters 7–8.

Revelation 15 and 16 introduce us to seven angels with seven bowls, which are the last in the series of plagues (15:1). The seven bowls, like the seven trumpets, are modeled on the plagues in Exodus.

Revelation 17 and 18 depict "the judgment of the great harlot" (17:1). Though there are several OT passages behind the imagery of the harlot (e.g., Isaiah 23–24, and 27, Jeremiah 50–51, and Ezekiel 26–28), the most significant is Ezekiel 16: "But you trusted in your beauty and played the harlot because of your fame, and you poured out your harlotries on every passer-by who might be willing. . . . You built yourself a high place at the top of every street and made your beauty abominable" (Ezek. 16:15, 25a). The harlot is described as world renowned (17:2; cf. Ezek. 16:15, 25), she is wearing jewels and fine linen (17:4; cf. Ezek. 16:13), and she is guilty of shedding blood (17:6; cf. Ezek. 16:38).

The final four chapters of Revelation (19–22) have a multitude of OT allusions. The most significant background for this section is Ezekiel 37–48. Both Ezekiel 37–48 and Revelation 19–22 describe the intrusion of Gog and Magog, a mighty battle, and the establishment of a temple/city where God's presence dwells among His people.

Revelation 19 opens with three hallelujahs (19:1, 3, 6), which contrasts the three groups who were weeping and mourning the demise of the harlot in chapter 18 (18:9, 11, 15–17). The hallelujahs are then followed by the announcement of the marriage supper of the Lamb (19:7–10). This supper certainly parallels the great end-times feast of Isaiah 24:21–25:10. Revelation 19 closes with an account of the birds being summoned to the "great supper of God" (19:17), where they will feast on the flesh of those who wage war against and are defeated by Christ. The OT background for this supper is Ezekiel 39:4, 17–20.

The significance of Ezekiel 37–48 for the book of Revelation intensifies as we reach Revelation 20–22. Revelation 20 narrates the binding of Satan, his release, the gathering of Gog and Magog for war, and the great white throne judgment. The reference to Gog and Magog clearly associates this section with Ezekiel 38–39, where Gog and Magog are the ultimate enemies who oppose God's people and are destroyed by God. With the background of Ezekiel 38–39 in view, John is able to assure his readers that the great enemies of God will be defeated.

Revelation 21–22 brings the story of Revelation to a climax. God's eternal temple/city will descend from heaven to the earth. Sin and death will be no more. It is here that God's glorious presence will dwell among His people forever (21:3, 11; cf. Ezek. 43:2–9).

The influence of Ezekiel 37–48 continues in the depiction of the new Jerusalem (21:9–22:5). In both passages the prophet (Ezekiel and John, respectively) is taken to a high place where they are shown the new city (21:10; Ezek. 40:2). Both see a figure with a measuring rod (21:15; Ezek. 40:3). In both accounts the city is actually a temple with three gates on each side, walls, and foundations (21:12–13; Ezek. 48:31–34). In both accounts living water flows out from the temple/throne (22:1–2; Ezek. 47:1–9). And in both accounts there is a tree (or trees in Ezekiel) whose leaves bring healing to the nations (22:2; Ezek. 47:12).

The most significant element of the new Jerusalem is the presence of God among His people. This is the fulfillment of the great hope of Ezekiel 37:27–28, which is itself a reiteration of the promise of Leviticus 26:11–12. Revelation 21:7 states, "I will be his God and he will be My son."

Of course, no survey on the centrality of the OT for understanding the book of Revelation would be complete without reference to the significance of the garden of Eden in Genesis 2–3. The book of Revelation confirms that in the end the hope of Eden is restored. As God dwelt with humankind in Eden (Gen. 3:8), so He will do so in the new creation (21:3–4). Just as Eden had gold of the highest quality (Gen. 2:11–12), a river (Gen. 2:10), and the tree of life (Gen. 3:9, 22), so also does the new Jerusalem (gold: 21:18; river: 22:1; tree of life: 22:2). In the new Jerusalem, the curse of Eden is removed: "There will no longer be any curse" (22:3).

HOW THE OLD TESTAMENT BACKGROUND INFORMS REVELATION

The abundance of OT passages that reside behind the imagery of the book of Revelation affirms that a proper reading of the book of Revelation must include an awareness of the OT background. Since the goal of this study is not to provide a comprehensive understanding of the book of Revelation but to help the reader understand the basic meaning of the book and how to interpret it for themselves, only a few examples will be offered here.

Revelation 11: The Two Witnesses

When we examine the account of the two witnesses (11:1–13), we quickly recognize that they are depicted in terms of the ministries of

Moses and Elijah—they have power to shut up the sky so that rain may not fall and to turn the waters into blood (11:6). It is important to note that Moses and Elijah were widely understood to represent the Law and the Prophets.[11] The two witnesses are thus described like Moses and Elijah because their witness is in accord with the entirety of the OT witness.[12] That they are *two* is likely because two is the number of credible witnesses. As a result, we might understand the mission of the two witnesses as faithfully proclaiming the Scriptures to the nations.

Revelation 12: The Dragon Pursues the Woman

In Revelation 12, the dragon (whom we are told is Satan [12:9]) opposes the woman's offspring (12:3), and pursues both the woman (12:13) and her offspring: "So the dragon was enraged with the woman, and went off to make war with the rest of her children, who keep the commandments of God and hold to the testimony of Jesus" (12:17).

This account alerts us that the people of God should not to be surprised when persecution comes. After all, the devil persecuted God's people in the OT world. Here John reminds us that the same dragon attempted to persecute Christ. And now we learn that the dragon persecutes "the rest of her offspring" (12:17)—the people of God today.

The narrative of the dragon and the woman confirms the notion that the book of Revelation is an exhortation for the people of God to overcome. John provides the narrative context for this charge: There is a dragon pursuing you!

---

11. "The Law and the Prophets" was a common way of referring to the entirety of the OT and this likely accounts for why Moses and Elijah were present at the transfiguration of Jesus (cf. Matt. 17:1–9; Mark 9:2–10; Luke 9:28–36). See Beale, *Revelation*, 573. For a discussion as to why John appears to depict them in terms of Moses and Elijah, see Richard Bauckham, *The Climax of Prophecy: Studies on the Book of Revelation* (Edinburgh: T&T Clark, 1993), 276–77.

12. Many readers are possibly imagining the presence of two individuals at this point. Though that is understandable from a modern point of view, it is doubtful that they are just two mere individuals. After all, part of the description of them says that they are two olives trees and two lampstands (11:4). We already know that lampstands represent churches and not individuals (1:20). This suggests that they are more than simply two individual persons. For a full discussion of the two witnesses, see my *Revelation and the Two Witnesses* (Eugene, OR: Wipf & Stock, 2011).

Revelation 14: The Two Harvests

A proper understanding of the biblical context and the distinction between the two harvests in Revelation 14 is significant for our ability to read and understand the book of Revelation.

The description of the first harvest (14:14–16) appears to be that of a grain harvest. It is important to note that a grain harvest only requires reaping. Thus we are told that "He who sat on the cloud swung His sickle over the earth, and the earth was reaped" (14:16). The act of harvesting alone is commonly associated with positive images.[13] John provides no indication here that judgment is included in this first harvest.[14]

The second harvest (14:17–20) is certainly a grape harvest. An angel tells the one who has the sickle, "Put in your sharp sickle and gather the clusters from the vine of the earth, because her grapes are ripe" (14:18). The narrative then confirms, "So the angel swung his sickle to the earth and gathered the clusters from the vine of the earth, and threw them into the great wine press of the wrath of God. And the wine press was trodden outside the city" (14:19–20a).

As noted above, the harvesting of the grapes appears to have Isaiah 63 as its primary background. Isaiah declares,

> Who is this who comes from Edom,
> With garments of glowing colors from Bozrah,
> This One who is majestic in His apparel,
> Marching in the greatness of His strength?
> "It is I who speak in righteousness, mighty to save."
> Why is Your apparel red,
> And Your garments like the one who treads in the wine press?
> "I have trodden the wine trough alone,
> And from the peoples there was no man with Me.
> I also trod them in My anger
> And trampled them in My wrath;

---

13. Cf. Mark 4:29; John 4:35–38.

14. When a grain harvest includes judgment, reference is commonly made to the inclusion of threshing and winnowing (cf. Pss. 1:4; 35:5; Isa. 17:13; 29:5; Jer. 51:33; Dan. 2:35; Hosea 13:3; Micah 4:12–13; Hab. 3:12; Matt. 3:12; Luke 3:17).

And their lifeblood is sprinkled on My garments,
And I stained all My raiment." (Isa. 63:1–3)

The context of Isaiah shows that the harvesting of grapes is one of God's judgment. The blood of His enemies has been trodden.

The readers of Revelation would undoubtedly have understood the harvest of grain as the harvest of the righteous. This comes not so much from the OT context as from Jesus' parable of the wheat and the tares:

> The one who sows the good seed is the Son of Man, and the field is the world; and as for the good seed, these are the sons of the kingdom; and the tares are the sons of the evil one; and the enemy who sowed them is the devil, and the harvest is the end of the age; and the reapers are angels. (Matt. 13:37–39)

In light of these biblical contexts, it appears that the grain harvest is that of the righteous and the grape harvest is that of judgment on the world.

CONCLUSION

This chapter has provided a foundation for understanding the imagery in the book of Revelation. Simply put, the imagery in the book of Revelation derives extensively from the biblical world, especially the OT. Recognizing the OT background behind the images of the book of Revelation is an important step in reading and understanding the book of Revelation.[15]

For Further Study

1. John's first description of the people of God in Revelation occurs in Revelation 1:6, where they are designated as "a kingdom" and "priests" (cf. also 5:10; 20:6; and 22:5). Now compare this with Exodus 19:4–6 and the key description of the people of God at Mount Sinai. What might this mean for our understanding of the book of Revelation and the role of the people of God today?

---

15. This shows us that there is something wrong with the claim that the proper background for understanding Revelation is instead our own modern context. See Appendix 1 for discussion.

2. Observe the use of the ten plagues in Egypt in the book of Revelation. Read Exodus 7:14–11:8 and then compare to the seven trumpets and the seven bowls (8:7–9:21; 11:15–19; 16:1–21). How many parallels can you find?

3. Compare the four beasts of Daniel 7:1–8 with the beast of Revelation 13:1–8. Note the parallels. What do you think is the significance of this for our understanding of the beast in Revelation 13?

4. Compare Ezekiel 37–48 and Revelation 19–22. List as many parallels between these passages as you can.[16] Note that the order of events in Ezekiel corresponds to the order in Revelation 19–22. What might this mean for understanding the book of Revelation?

5. What is the possible importance of the fact that Daniel 12:5–13, which is similar to Revelation 10:1–11, also has an angelic figure with a scroll? A key difference between the two accounts is that Daniel is told that the scroll is to remain "sealed" (Dan. 12:9), while John is told that he is not to seal up the book (22:10). In light of our study in this chapter, what is the possible significance of this?

Application

1. One important element in the narrative of the book of Revelation and its relationship to the OT is found in the fact that the new Jerusalem (21:1–22:5) has several key parallels with the garden of Eden in Genesis 2. That the Bible begins and ends with God's presence among His people in a garden should impact our understanding of the entire biblical narrative. What is the significance of this for our understanding of the Bible and for Christian living today?

---

16. Hint: note that each describes a city, which is a temple, which is also the people of God.

Conclusion to Part 1

Follow the Lamb! If you learn anything from this study, may it be that we are called to follow the Lamb. I hope that this book will also help you understand more fully what it means to follow the Lamb. This opening part of our study has provided insights that facilitate our understanding of the book of Revelation.

First, we have seen that *the Lamb is none other than the eternal God of all creation who has manifested Himself.* Christ has lived, died, and been resurrected. He is the One who is worthy to receive all worship. He is the Lion of the tribe of Judah. And just as significant as all these titles are, He is also the Lamb who was slain.

We, the people of God, are called to do what He did. That is, we are to persevere as faithful witnesses for the kingdom of God. The book of Revelation informs us that this will not be an easy task, but just as Jesus overcame, so shall we.

Second, we have seen that *the OT is the primary source for the imagery of the book of Revelation.* This has significant implications for how we read Revelation. At the same time, I can see many readers of this book concluding that this is a difficult task for them. After all, many Christians today are simply not familiar with the OT—certainly not well enough to discern when John is using it. I want to assure the reader that this is quite fine. My goal for this part of the book is not to ask my readers to be able to discern the OT context for each of the images in the book of Revelation. Instead, the goal is simply to alert you that there is such a context. The importance of this is that we learn not to run after some contemporary event(s) and see in them Revelation's fulfillment, as though the images were pointing forward to something in the twenty-first century. Instead, we should learn to look to the OT for our understanding of these images.

If we combine these two features of the book of Revelation, we have the primary keys to understanding it—namely, that the book of Revelation is about Jesus in light of His fulfillment of the OT promises. For many readers, this is where the excitement of the book of Revelation resides. We have a lifetime to continue to uncover the riches embedded in the book of Revelation. And we do so by mining the book for its teachings about Jesus.

If we were to stop reading this book at this point and to read Revelation in light of the principle that it is about Jesus and our call to imitate Him, we would do quite well. But there is more—much more. And it only gets better from here!

PART 2

Secondary Keys to Reading Revelation Effectively

Introduction to Part 2

Part 1 has laid a necessary foundation for reading, understanding, and applying the book of Revelation. If one read only Part 1 of this book and did not
proceed into Part 2 and beyond, one would still do well when it comes to interpreting the book of Revelation. At the same time, however, one would miss so
much. In Part 2 we will begin to look at other features that will further equip
us to read Revelation more effectively. Now the real fun begins.

The book of Revelation is an intricate work with incredible beauty. It
appears that John has carefully constructed his story in such a way that
perceptive readers might continue to unveil key elements of the book. The
result is that the deeper we dig into the book of Revelation and its story
the more treasure we find.

Now I am not suggesting that one needs a secret decoder ring, or some
magical formula that is only available to us in the twenty-first century. Or
that if you mail in $50 I will send you a special prayer blanket that you
lay on top of the Bible and the meaning suddenly seeps into your minds.

Instead, in this part of our study we will look at the masterful way in
which John has penned his book so that the careful reader will continue
to discern its powerful message. We will begin in chapter 5 with a look at
John's use of numbers. Many of the numbers are in plain view. There are
seven seals, seven trumpets, and seven bowls. There are twenty-four elders.
The walls of the new Jerusalem are 144 cubits thick.[17] And the number

---

17. It is here that a good translation is needed. Because numbers are so vital to
understanding the book of Revelation, as we will see in the following chapter, it is essential
for translations not to cover them up.

of the beast is 666. Others, however, are more intricately woven into the fabric of the book. We will learn that John has carefully written this book to reflect the significance of certain numbers. As a result, numbers are central to the book of Revelation and discerning their significance is vital to a proper reading of the book of Revelation today

Though many might be skeptical (and understandably so), we will note that the sheer frequency and consistency in which key words, phrases, and titles occur a specific number of times confirms that this is no accident. As we will see, John has intentionally constructed his writing so that the readers are invited to discern the numerical significance within the book of Revelation.

Next, in chapter 6 we will look at the various genres (or styles of writings) that John has used. One of the most difficult aspects of the book of Revelation for many modern readers is that John uses three genres: letter, prophecy, and apocalyptic. Add to this the fact that these genres are ancient in nature and do not conform to any contemporary writing styles and we recognize the difficulty in understanding the book of Revelation. Therefore, it is essential to provide a basic understanding of the nature of ancient letters, prophecy, and apocalyptic literature in order to understand Revelation today.

CHAPTER 5

John's Use of Numbers

The book of Revelation is a beautifully written document. The presence of numbers in the book of Revelation is apparent to even a casual reader. Revelation is replete with sevens and twelves and tens. While it is likely that some of these features of Revelation may not have been noticed by the original hearers on a first reading,[1] they are still not likely to be accidents. There are just too many occurrences for them to be labeled as happenstance.

John's use of numbers, however, reaches even deeper than this. It appears that John has constructed his work in such a manner that key words and phrases appear a specific number of times. For example, the word "blessed" occurs seven times in the book of Revelation (1:3; 14:13; 16:15; 19:9; 20:6; 22:7, 14). In light of the significance of the number seven, one would be hard pressed to contend that the presence of "blessed" seven times in the book is not of some importance.[2]

---

1. Though I would not underestimate the interpretive skills of the original audience. They were much more adept at reading (or hearing) apocalypses than we are.

2. When it comes to the idea that numbers play a significant role in the book of Revelation, or any part of Scripture for that matter, many readers are highly suspicious and rightfully so. Truth be told, I used to be one of the most ardent skeptics when it came to numbers and the Bible. After all, it seemed as though the so-called prophecy experts all had a different conclusion as to what each number supposedly represented. Not only that, many set forth wild speculations as to the importance of the various numbers—all of which led to some very fanciful, and subsequently wrong, interpretations. A careful study of Revelation will show, however, that numbers indeed play a consistent and significant role in the book.

The key is that John consistently used certain numbers in such a way that he intended for his readers to see in them an added depth of meaning to his work. Examining John's use of numbers, the most significant of which are three, four, seven, and twelve (and the multiples of them), provides strong confirmation of this assertion.

A careful study of the book of Revelation confirms that Revelation is an incredibly intricate work in which numbers play a key role in John's construction and, thereby, in the interpretation of the book. In fact, if it is true that John has intentionally written in such a way that there is a deeper, richer meaning in the text, then we would be remiss if we failed to account for such in our reading of the book. That is, if John used numbers in such a manner that he intended for us to count the number of times a given word or phrase appears, then our understanding of the book would be incomplete unless we did so.

To be clear: John's use of numbers is not of first importance. One can read and understand the book of Revelation and its meaning without realizing the important role that numbers play in the construction of the book; we can see that the book is about Jesus and His victory through His death and resurrection and our call to imitate Him without ever noticing the role of numbers. John's use of numbers does, however, serve to enrich, intensify, and deepen our understanding of the text.

EXAMINING IMPORTANT NUMBERS IN THE BOOK OF REVELATION

Four

The number four is consistently used throughout the book of Revelation to symbolically represent completeness in relation to the creation and the world. This likely derives from the fact that the world naturally has four primary directions. Consequently, in the book of Revelation the earth has four corners and four winds: "After this I saw four angels standing at the four corners of the earth, holding back the four winds of the earth" (7:1; cf. 20:8).

We see, then, that throughout the book of Revelation the world is consistently divided into four portions: "Fear God, and give Him glory, because the hour of His judgment has come; worship Him who made the heaven and the earth and sea and springs of waters" (14:7).

This may provide some insight into the significance of the fact that the divine description "who lives for ever and ever" (4:9, 10; 10:6; 15:7) occurs four times. Does John use this title to designate God as sovereign over creation? That such is the case gains credence from the fact that God is acknowledged as the creator immediately following the first two occurrences of this title (4:11).

In addition, the book of Revelation commonly refers to the people of the world (often, though not always, in contrast to the people of God) by means of a fourfold designation: "It was also given to him to make war with the saints and to overcome them, and authority over every tribe and people and tongue and nation was given to him" (13:7). Although the order of the titles varies through the book of Revelation, the people of the world are consistently referred to with a fourfold designation. For example, Revelation 14:6 says, "And I saw another angel flying in midheaven, having an eternal gospel to preach to those who live on the earth, and to every nation and tribe and tongue and people."

In addition to this, we find that John refers to the people of the world with a fourfold designation a total of seven times (5:9; 7:9; 10:11; 11:9; 13:7; 14:6; 17:15). It is recognized that John varies the order of words in each occurrence, and he even substitutes a different word on two occasions. Nonetheless, what is consistent is the fact that every reference to the people of the world has four terms and that there are seven such references.

Since the number four is commonly used to indicate completion in regard to the creation and the world, it appears that John refers to the people of the world by means of a fourfold designation in order to inform his readers that he is referring to all the people of the world—though on most occasions this group does not include those whose names are found written in the book of life, a fact that John makes clear in Revelation 13:

> It was also given to him to make war with the saints and to overcome them, and authority over every tribe and people and tongue and nation was given to him. All who dwell on the earth will worship him, everyone whose name has not been written from the foundation of the world in the book of life of the Lamb who has been slain (13:7–8).

Three

Though the number three appears to have a variety of uses, it is consistently applied to God in the book of Revelation. This accords with the Scriptural designation of God as Trinity—Father, Son, and Spirit. Throughout the book of Revelation, we find that certain titles for God have a threefold element to them. For example, God is "the one who is and who was and who is to come" (1:4, 8; 4:8). It is interesting to note that this threefold title occurs three times (though in 4:8 the order is different). It is also intriguing that this designation occurs two other times but not in a threefold manner. For example, Revelation 11:17 says, "We give You thanks, O Lord God, the Almighty, who are and who were." Revelation 16:5 similarly says, "Righteous are You, who are and who were, O Holy One." Notice that these two verses omit "and who is to come." This leads us to consider the fact that perhaps these passages do not include this statement because at this point in the narrative He has come.[3]

Other important titles for God and Christ also occur with a threefold designation. Thus, God is the "Alpha and Omega, the first and last, the beginning and end" (22:13). This threefold title appears in various forms throughout the book. The single designation of God as the "Alpha and the Omega" appears three times (1:8; 21:6; 22:13). It is worth noting that the total occurrences of the differing titles are seven: "Alpha and Omega" (three times), "first and last" (1:17; 22:13: two times), and "beginning and the end" (21:6; 22:13: two times).

The use of the number three in relation to God is further present in the threefold proclamation of the four living creatures, who declare God to be "HOLY, HOLY, HOLY" (4:8). In addition, in praising God they use a threefold designation for God is to receive: "Worthy are You, our Lord and our God, to receive glory and honor and power" (4:11).

The number three is also significant in the depiction of Jesus. As noted earlier, the first mention of Christ in the book of Revelation includes the threefold designation of "the faithful witness, the firstborn from the dead, and the ruler of the kings of the earth" (1:5).

---

3. I will discuss this point further in chapter 7. This conclusion, of course, raises the question of whether or not the book of Revelation is laid out in a strictly linear fashion or if there is some cyclical element to it. If one concludes that it is strictly linear, then it would be hard to conclude that God has come as early as Revelation 11.

Finally, we also observe that the number three also occurs in regard to Satan and his accomplices. This raises the question as to why John would use numbers that are reserved for God when referring to evil. The answer likely resides in the fact that the book of Revelation portrays Satan as the great imitator of God.

We find, then, that Satan (or "the dragon," as he is called in 12:9) has two accomplices: the beast (13:1–8) and the false prophet (13:11–18).[4] Together with Satan they are widely considered to form a satanic trinity. Of course, the reader is easily clued in to the fact that, though they attempt to mimic God and appear as God, they are clearly not.

This satanic trinity appears most directly in Revelation 16:13: "And I saw coming out of the mouth of the dragon and out of the mouth of the beast and out of the mouth of the false prophet, three unclean spirits like frogs." Revelation chapters 19 and 20 go on to describe the judgment of this false trinity. The judgment concludes, "And the devil who deceived them was thrown into the lake of fire and brimstone, where the beast and the false prophet are also" (20:10).

With this being said, it is also important to note that the beast, who parodies Christ,[5] is also referred to with an ironic threefold designation: "The beast that you saw was, and is not, and is about to come up" (17:8). Interestingly, this threefold ironic designation occurs three times (17:8 [twice], 11). This seems to confirm for us that John intends for us to understand the beast as the one who attempts to mimic God: "the one who is and who was and who is to come" (1:4, 8; 4:8).

The reader of the book of Revelation should not be fooled. It seems as though John makes it obvious to the reader that Satan and his minions are only imitators of Christ. But the fact that these beings are described in a manner that is reserved for God makes us wonder: Does John intend to warn us that in reality we may well be deceived by the devil and his minions? That is, does John want us to be aware of the insidious nature of the beast and the false prophet because in reality we are in danger or temptation of being deceived by them? Do not be fooled, warns John, the

---

4. Note that second beast is called the "false prophet" in 16:13. See below for further discussion.

5. We will examine the notion that Satan and his minions imitate and parody Christ in chapter 10.

beast "who had the wound of the sword and has come to life" (13:14) is not Christ—he is a seven-headed and ten-horned hybrid monster who is empowered by the dragon. The world will follow this beast (13:8), but the people of God must recognize him for who he is.

Seven

Seven is one of the most consistently used numbers in the entire Bible. The symbolic significance of this number extends beyond the apocalyptic literature of the Bible. Even in the book of Genesis we find a consistent use of the number seven.[6] It is not surprising then to find that the number seven pervades the book of Revelation. In the book of Revelation, and the whole of Scripture, seven most commonly represents completion and perfection, especially as it relates to God.

Seven and the Father

The number seven is used in a variety of ways in relation to God. One way is that important divine names or titles occur seven times.[7] For instance, the title "Lord God, the Almighty" is found in Revelation 1:8; 4:8; 11:17; 15:3; 16:7; 19:6; 21:22. Though the order of words varies slightly in these seven passages, the fact that the threefold designation of "Lord," "God," and "the Almighty" is present seven times is clearly important.

Seven and Jesus

Since Jesus is the manifestation of God, it should come as no surprise that the title "Christ" occurs seven times in the book of Revelation (1:1, 2, 5; 11:15; 12:10; 20:4, 6).

In light of the fact that John's description of Jesus as "the faithful witness" (1:5) is central to the book of Revelation, it is also quite fascinating to observe that the name "Jesus" appears fourteen times (7 x 2—1:1, 2, 5, 9 [twice]; 12:17; 14:12; 17:6; 19:10 [twice]; 20:4; 22:16, 20, 21). Why fourteen times? We know that seven means perfection and completion,

---

6. Numbers are actually quite important to the construction of many books of the Bible, including Genesis. The most obvious example is the seven days of creation in Genesis 1–2. There are less apparent examples as well, including the fact that the list of the descendants of Jacob who travel to Egypt were "seventy" (Gen. 46:27).

7. See Richard Bauckham, *The Theology of the Book of Revelation* (Cambridge: Cambridge University Press, 1993), 33–37.

but why would John multiply it by two in the presentation of the name "Jesus"?

The answer appears to be that throughout the Scriptures the number two is used to represent the number of credible witnesses. This derives from the Deuteronomic principle "On the evidence of two witnesses or three witnesses, he who is to die shall be put to death; he shall not be put to death on the evidence of one witness" (Deut. 17:6).[8] It is in accord with the principle of a trustworthy witness that the name "Jesus" occurs fourteen times: He is the perfect and faithful witness. This conclusion gains further support in the book of Revelation from the fact that of the fourteen occurrences of "Jesus," seven of them are in conjunction with either the word "witness" or "testimony" (1:2, 9; 12:17; 17:6; 19:10 [twice]; 20:4).

Another significant title for Jesus is "the Lamb." The book of Revelation refers to Jesus as "the Lamb" twenty-eight times (7 x 4).[9] Why twenty-eight times? The significance of this may well derive from the importance of Jesus as the Lamb of God in relation to the nations: "Worthy are You to take the book and to break its seals; for You were slain, and purchased for God with Your blood men from every tribe and tongue and people and nation. . . . Worthy is the Lamb that was slain" (5:9, 12). Jesus is the Lamb. The Lamb is the redeemer of the world. Since the number four is used with regard to the nations of the world, it is only fitting that the book of Revelation refers to Jesus as "the Lamb" twenty-eight times. This conclusion is strengthened by the fact that the first occurrence of the fourfold designation for nations of the world occurs in Revelation 5 where Jesus is introduced as the Lamb who is worthy to take the book and to break it seals because He is the one who "purchased for God with Your blood men from every tribe and tongue and people and nation" (5:9).

In addition to this we see that seven is also used explicitly in John's description of the Lamb. John tells us that the Lamb has "seven horns

---

8. Cf. Deuteronomy 19:15. Note that this principle likely influenced the ministry of Jesus and His sending the disciples out in pairs: Luke 10:2; cf. Luke 9:1-6; 10:1-16; Matthew 10:1-15. This is a feature that continues in the ministry of Paul when he chooses Barnabas and later Silas as his traveling companions (Acts 13:2-3; 15:40).

9. The word "lamb" occurs twenty-eight times in reference to Jesus (5:6, 8, 12, 13; 6:1, 16; 7:9, 10, 14, 17; 12:11; 13:8; 14:1, 4 [twice], 10; 15:3; 17:14 [twice]; 19:7, 9; 21:9, 14, 22, 23; 21:27; 22:1, 3), and it is used once in connection with the beast from the sea who has "horns like a lamb" (13:11).

and seven eyes, which are the seven Spirits of God, sent out into all the earth" (5:6). Again, we notice the importance of the Lamb in relation to the world.

Seven and the Spirit

The word "spirit/Spirit" seems to occur fourteen times in reference to the Holy Spirit.[10] The significance of fourteen, which is again likely the result of seven times two—with seven representing perfection and completion and two representing the number of trustworthy witnesses—may be found in the statement in 19:10, where we see that "the testimony of Jesus is the spirit of prophecy."

In addition, four of these references are to "the seven Spirits of God" (1:4; 3:1; 4:5; 5:6).[11] The four references to the seven spirits is explained by the fact that four indicates the created realm and the Spirit is the One who is "sent out into all the earth" (5:6). The significance of the fact that there are four occurrences of "the seven Spirits" may well be that it is the Spirit who empowers the people of God to be effective witnesses to the world.

Other Uses of Seven

I have already noted the importance of seven as a number that reflects perfection and completion and one that is especially worthy of God. The book of Revelation is saturated with explicit indications of the number seven: there are seven churches,[12] seals,[13] trumpets,[14] bowls,[15] and beatitudes,[16]

---

10. Cf. 1:4; 2:7, 11, 17, 29; 3:1, 6, 13, 22; 4:5; 5:6; 14:13; 19:10; 22:17. There are a couple of questionable uses of "spirit" that may refer to the Holy Spirit (e.g., 11:11; 22:6).

11. The use of "seven Spirits" to refer to the Holy Spirit is a matter of small debate. That it refers to the Holy Spirit is the common understanding. The fact that the number seven is used for God in the book of Revelation provides some support for this conclusion. In addition, that the first occurrence of "seven Spirits" is in 1:4 also supports the understanding that John has the Holy Spirit in mind. After all, the reference to the "seven Spirits" is sandwiched between a clear reference to the Father and to Jesus: "Grace to you and peace, from Him who is and who was and who is to come, and from the seven Spirits who are before His throne, and from Jesus Christ" (1:4–5). That this is an allusion to the Holy Spirit is reflected in the NLT translation of "seven Spirits" as "sevenfold Spirit."

12. 1:4, 11, 20; 2–3.

13. 5:1; 6:1–8:1.

14. 8:2, 6–9:21; 11:15.

15. 16:1–21.

16. 1:3; 14:13; 16:15; 19:9; 20:6; 22:7, 14.

and a dragon with seven heads.[17] In addition to the examples mentioned above, the number seven appears embedded in the text so that words such as "prophecy"[18] and "come"[19] occur seven times. We also find God worshiped with seven accolades.[20]

Twelve

Throughout the Scriptures in general, and the book of Revelation in particular, the number twelve represents completion and totality, especially in regard to the people of God. This basic meaning for the number twelve continues in the book of Revelation. Consequently, in the book of Revelation we find that there are twelve tribes (7:4–8; 21:12) and twelve apostles (21:14). In addition to this there are twenty-four elders (12 x 2—4:4, 10; 5:8; 11:16; 19:4). It is widely recognized, though not universally agreed upon, that the twenty-four elders represent the combined group of the OT and NT people of God—perhaps more specifically, the twenty-four elders are the twelve patriarchs (representing the twelve tribes) and the twelve apostles.

The use of the number twelve in reference to the people of God accounts for the abundant use of twelve in the description of the new Jerusalem (21:1–22:5). The new Jerusalem, which on the surface appears to be a city (3:12; 21:2), is also the bride/people of God (21:9–10).[21] There is a close correspondence between the city and the people of God. The city has twelve gates (21:12–13), upon which are written the names of the twelve tribes (21:12). The city has twelve foundation stones (21:14), upon which are the names of the twelve apostles (21:14). Here again we see the combination of the twelve tribes and the twelve apostles.

An additional use of twelve in the description of the new Jerusalem includes the fact that the length, width, and height of the city are each twelve

---

17. 12:3.

18. 1:3; 11:6; 19:10; 22:7, 10, 18, 19.

19. 6:1, 3, 5, 7; 22:1 (twice), 20.

20. 5:12: "power and riches and wisdom and might and honor and glory and dominion"; 7:12: "blessing and glory and wisdom and thanksgiving and honor and power and might."

21. In 21:9 John is told that he is going to be shown the bride, but in 21:10 he is shown "the holy city." This is best understood in such a way that the city is the bride. See chapter 10 for further discussion.

thousand stadia (21:16), or about fifteen hundred miles.[22] Furthermore, the wall of the city is 144 (12 x 12) cubits thick (21:17).[23] The city is also adorned with twelve different precious stones (21:19–20), which are said to comprise "every kind of precious stone" (21:19). In the midst of the city is the tree of life, which itself bears "twelve kinds of fruit" (22:2).

The number twelve, then, is consistently used in reference to the people of God and the glory that awaits them in the new Jerusalem. The consistent use of the number twelve in the description of the new Jerusalem provides further support for the claim that the city corresponds to the people of God.

Three and a Half

The number three and a half is also worth mentioning here because of its importance in the book of Revelation. We must note that its meaning is far from clear. The significance of this number likely derives from its presence in the OT, in particular the book of Daniel and other apocalyptic writings. In general, the number three and a half occurs in this literature to indicate the period of time in which the people of God suffer.[24]

This time frame itself appears most prominently in the book of Daniel. Daniel 7:25 states, "He will speak out against the Most High and wear down the saints of the Highest One, and he will intend to make alterations in times and in law; and they will be given into his hand for a time, times,

---

22. The NASB uses "fifteen hundred miles" in the text and places "Lit., twelve thousand stadia" in the footnotes. This is likely because the translators surmised that most readers are not familiar with stadia. In light of the symbolic significance of numbers in the book of Revelation, this is not the best way to translate the verse. Since numbers are central to a proper understanding of the book of Revelation, translations of Revelation should be very careful in how they translate them. The ESV and the NIV both translate it as "twelve thousand stadia." The importance here is not so much the length of a stadium, but that it was twelve thousand of them, which is 12 x 1,000.

23. The NASB translates it "seventy-two yards" with a footnote that reads, "Lit., one hundred forty-four cubits." Here also the importance is not how long a cubit is (typically considered a foot and a half, or the span from the tip of the average person's longest finger to the elbow), but that it was 144 of them (as reflected in the ESV, NIV, and NET translations), which is 12 x 12.

24. Bauckham, *Climax of Prophecy*, 400–404. We must exercise more caution when it comes to numbers such as three and a half. The fact that this designation does not occur as often as the numbers three, four, seven, and twelve itself means that we do not have as many examples to draw conclusions from.

and half a time."[25] What could Daniel be referring to when he says that the saints will be worn down for "a time, times, and half a time"? The difficulty for understanding the meaning of "time, times, and half a time" stems from the fact that the second term, "times," is undefined—as a result, it could refer to two, three, a billion, or any number of times.

It may well be that John uses this designation in order to illuminate Daniel's time frame. John, who uses the Danielic time frame of "a time, times, and half a time" in Revelation 12:14, also uses other expressions that appear to more clearly specify three-and-one-half. For example, in 11:2 and 13:5, he uses "forty-two months." And in 11:3 and 12:6, he uses "1,260." Since the time frames of "a time, times, and half a time" (12:14) and "1,260 days" refer to the same period, it appears that John has provided us with clarity as to his use of Daniel's "a time, times, and half a time." After all, both forty-two months and 1,260 days equate to three-and-one-half on a Jewish calendar.[26]

The notion that three-and-one-half years provides the time frame for the suffering of the people of God fits well with its apparent use in the book of Revelation. It appears that in 13:5–7 three-and-one-half years serves as the time frame for the beast's reign of terror against the people of God.

The significance and meaning of three-and-one-half years as the period in which the people of God suffer is hard to determine. Perhaps it lies in the fact that three-and-one-half is the number seven divided in half. It is interesting to note that the Gospels may indicate that Jesus' ministry was three-and-one-half years. Could it be that the perfect reign of God would be seven years? Does the NT intend to indicate that Jesus ministered for three-and-one-half years and was "cut off"[27] and now the NT people of God minister for an additional three-and-one-half years? If so, the combined reigns of Christ and His people would constitute a seven.

Other Numbers

Certain other numbers also play a role in the book of Revelation. Most notable among them is the number two. As mentioned above, the number

---

25. This designation also appears in Daniel 12:7.

26. A Jewish calendar at the time of John consisted of 360 days. In order to keep with the seasons they simply added another thirty-day month at the end of every sixth year.

27. An expression used in the highly debated passage of Daniel 9:24–27.

two is used for the number of credible or true witnesses. This is likely the significance of the two witnesses in 11:1–13.

The number ten appears to designate completion especially as it relates to the law. This is apparent in the Scriptures by the presence of the Ten Commandments. The number ten appears in several places in Revelation. Most notably, both the dragon and the beast are said to have ten horns (12:3; 13:1; 17:3, 7). Could it be that the ten horns represent civil power and authority? This is supported by the fact that John is told that the beast has ten diadems on his horns (13:1) and that John is told that "the ten horns which you saw are ten kings" (17:12; cf. 17:16).

The number six does not have any importance in and of itself. It does appear to gain significance, though, by means of a contrast with the number seven. If seven represents completion and perfection then six, falling one short of seven, may connote incompleteness and imperfection. This may be the importance of the famed 666—namely, that it indicates a satanic trinity that comes short of 777.[28]

CONCLUSION

It is understandable that many readers of the book of Revelation today are hesitant to see a symbolic significance to the numbers in the book of Revelation. Ascribing significance to numbers appears subjective and speculative. The sheer abundance and consistency with which John uses numbers, however, confirms that ascribing significance to his use of numbers is neither subjective nor speculative.

In most instances, the meaning and significance of the numbers is apparent. Seven represents completion and perfection. Four represents completion especially as it relates to the creation. Three indicates completion as it relates to God. Twelve signifies completion as it relates to the people of God. Since three represents God, it is appropriate that God is worshiped by an unending chorus of "Holy, Holy, Holy." Since twelve represents the people of God, it is appropriate that the number twelve is abundant in the description of the new Jerusalem.

---

28. Though there is a legitimate question as to whether the original text read "616" or "666," the evidence strongly favors "666." See Beale, *Revelation*, 718–28; Bauckham, *Climax of Prophecy*, 384–407.

Interestingly, we find that significant numbers for God are used in relation to evil. These instances may be accounted for as examples of parody. The dragon and the beast may have seven heads (cf. 12:3; 13:1), but the reader is keenly aware that they are forces of evil. That they have seven heads may be accounted for, then, by the fact that they are imitating God and the Lamb. The use of important numbers for evil does not negate our conclusions regarding John's use of numbers; rather, it supports it.[29] The dragon may have seven heads, but we all know that he does not represent the true king of the earth—he is, after all, a dragon.

In order to understand the book of Revelation more fully we must consider how numbers expand our understanding of the book. It is important to reiterate that we learned nothing new in terms of the message of the book of Revelation. John's use of numbers highlight, accent, and intensify features of the book that were already discernible to readers.

From all this it is apparent that John weighed nearly every word before he penned his final work. And the discovery of such a fact makes the study of the book of Revelation even more enjoyable.

For Further Study

1. Revelation 2–3 has seven letters to seven churches. In light of the significance of the number seven in Scripture and in the book of Revelation, what do you think is the importance of there being seven churches?

2. Note that the title "Christ" appears seven times in the book of Revelation (1:1, 2, 5; 11:15; 12:10; 20:4, 6). What is the significance of this?

3. Note that the name "Jesus" is used seven times in connection with the expression "testimony"/"witness" (1:2, 9; 12:17; 17:6; 19:10[twice]; 20:4). What is the significance of this?

4. The word "mark" occurs seven times (13:16, 17; 14:9, 11; 16:2; 19:20; 20:4). Compare and contrast the use of the term in each occurrence and determine the possible significance of this term.

---

29. This accords with the NT affirmations that Satan appears as "angel of light" (2 Cor. 11:14) and that false prophets will come "in sheep's clothing" (Matt. 7:15).

5. The word "come" occurs seven times (6:1, 3, 5, 7; 22:17[twice], 20). What is the possible significance of this?

6. The description of God as one "who lives forever and ever" occurs four times (4:9, 10; 10:6; 15:7). What is the possible significance of this?

7. Read the account of the new Jerusalem (21:9–22:5) and observe how often the number twelve occurs. Note the measurements of the city in the NKJV of 21:16, 17.

8. In the judgment of the grape harvest in Revelation 14 it is said that the blood comes out of the winepress for a distance of sixteen hundred stadia (14:20). What is the possible significance of sixteen hundred stadia?[30]

9. Understanding John's use of numbers is critical when we look at such matters as the two witnesses of Revelation 11. Read 11:1–13 carefully. What might be the significance of the fact that they are two witnesses?[31]

10. What is the significance of the fact that the two witnesses are the "two olive trees and the two lampstands" (11:4)? Note that in order to answer this question well it is important to determine any OT context and how this might impact our understanding. In this instance, the OT context would be Zechariah 4:1–6. It is also important to discern how the imagery is used in the book of Revelation. For lampstands, of course, note 1:20.

11. List reasons why the two witnesses could be considered to be two individuals and why they could be representatives of a larger body.

Application

1. What do you suppose might be the significance of the fact that Revelation is so intricately written? Does this reflect at all on the sovereignty of God?

---

30. Hint: sixteen hundred may well be derived from 4 x 4 x 10 x 10.
31. Hint: note the OT significance of two witnesses in Deuteronomy 19:15 and 17:6.

CHAPTER 6

Understanding Genre and Revelation

I had a professor tell me that he thought that the best interpreters of the book of Revelation were children. Children, he noted, just seem to get it. They read the account of Revelation 12 and know the following intuitively: dragon—bad; woman clothed with the sun—good; dragon pursuing the woman—bad; eagle rescues the woman—good; dragon tries to drown the woman—bad; earth swallows the water and the woman is rescued—good; dragon then chases the woman and her offspring—uh oh!

Many adults, on the other hand, especially those raised in certain evangelical traditions, read the book of Revelation and attempt to decode everything. They get carried away with attempts to identify the exact referents of the dragon's ten horns and the beast's seven heads.

This brings us to the issue of genre, that is, the style of writing. Genre asks the questions as to how the work at hand is to be read: Shall we understand it as history, poetry, a legend, a personal letter, or something else? Discerning the genre and how that genre works is essential for a proper reading of the book of Revelation—or any piece of literature for that matter.

In many instances, we intuitively understand the nature of a writing. When we read the front page of a newspaper and learn of a loss we, are grieved. We are saddened but not grieved when we learn of a loss in the sports page. We intuitively know that winning and losing means one thing on the front page and another in the sports page—and yet another in the obituary column. When we read the words "Once upon a time" at the opening of a fairy tale, we know what is going to happen: A princess will fall into distress and be rescued by a prince and they will live happily ever after; and we know that it is not a historical account.

Genre is essential to understanding any piece of literature. It is the genre that will help us discern whether John wanted us to read Revelation as "dragon is bad," or if we are to decode what the seven heads and ten horns might mean, or if there is another approach that we must take.

THE GENRES OF THE BOOK OF REVELATION

The difficulty with genre in the book of Revelation is twofold. First, Revelation is comprised of three genres: epistle (or letter), prophecy, and apocalypse. Second, for the most part, the genres of the book of Revelation are simply not familiar enough to most modern readers—even the nature of an epistle does not correspond fully to our modern letter writing (which itself is becoming a lost art with the advent of electronic mail). It is necessary, then, to have a foundational knowledge of these three genres in order to grasp some of the basic elements of the book of Revelation.

An important element for understanding genre in Revelation is that the genres used by John—epistle, prophecy, and apocalypse—were relevant to the people of his day. In fact, it is important to be reminded that all the books of the Bible were originally penned to particular groups; for example, Philippians was written to the church at Philippi, and 1 Timothy was written to Timothy, etc.[1] As such it is important to observe that they were concerned with conveying a message to the people to whom they were written. Certainly they do have an abiding significance through the ages to the present day, but they had, as their *primary* context, the audience to whom they were written. The book of Revelation was deeply rooted in its first-century context—John was writing to seven churches (1:4).

In addition to this, a fundamental assumption is that the book of Revelation had meaning to its original hearers. This may be controversial for some. But the simple fact is that with every other book of the New Testament we must first attempt to discern what it meant to its original readers.

Some might contend that Revelation is different because it is a prophecy and prophecy is always best understood after it has been fulfilled. There are

---

1. This is true even if we do not know precisely who the original audience was—e. g., Hebrews.

several problems with this line of thinking. First, Revelation is not simply a prophecy. It is also a letter and an apocalypse. Second, this suggestion fails to understand prophecy well. Third, though one might contend that this is the case with regard to the OT prophecies, it does not hold up well in the NT. The reason some aspects of OT prophecies were not understood is because Christ and the Spirit had not come. But this is not true for a NT prophecy; we do have Christ and the Spirit.

Thus in order to interpret the book of Revelation well it is essential to discern the various genres that John used and how his first readers would have understood his writing.

Letter

The easiest place to begin when it comes to the issue of genre in the book of Revelation is with its epistolary framework. Simply put, an epistle is an ancient letter. The book of Revelation, though not itself truly a letter, was written with an epistolary framework. That is, the book of Revelation's opening and closing display characteristics of an ancient letter.

The epistolary elements of the book of Revelation are most apparent in the opening chapters. Revelation begins like an ancient letter: "John to the seven churches that are in Asia: Grace to you and peace" (1:4). The author first identifies himself—John (cf. 1:4, 9). He then identifies the letter's recipients—the seven churches of Asia.[2] The seven churches are even named in 1:11 (Ephesus, Smyrna, Pergamum, Thyatira, Sardis, Philadelphia, and Laodicea), and each is addressed briefly in Revelation chapters 2 and 3.

The book of Revelation also has a somewhat formal epistolary ending: "The grace of the Lord Jesus be with all. Amen" (22:21). Though this scant reference is hardly enough to claim that the book of Revelation is a letter, when combined with the more formal opening, we see that there is indeed an epistolary frame for the book of Revelation.

Revelation, of course, is not purely a letter. In fact, aside from the seven letters of chapters 2 and 3, the rest of the book of Revelation does not read as an epistle. Even the seven letters of chapters 2 and 3 only have a few features in common with ancient epistles.

---

2. As stated previously, Asia was a province in the Roman Empire that comprised much of what is today western Turkey.

Recognizing that the book of Revelation has an epistolary framework, even if it is not an ancient letter in all respects, though, helps to remind us of its place in the first century. A letter is a communication from one person (in this case John) or group to another (in this case the seven churches of Asia). Letters are written because the author wants to convey a message to his or her readers. An important element, then, for determining what the message of the book might be for the church today must begin by discerning what John was trying to communicate to his original audience.

Prophecy

The book of Revelation declares itself to be a prophecy.[3] "Blessed is he who reads and those who hear the words of the prophecy, and heed the things which are written in it" (1:3).[4] The difficulty here is that the purpose of prophecy and the nature of prophetic language is commonly misunderstood today. Too often it is assumed that prophecy is a communication from God concerning the future. Instead, as with letters, prophecy was written at a moment in history in which the author intended primarily to convey a message to the people to whom he was writing in order to get them to act.[5] Thus prophecy was much more concerned with the prophet's own present world than with predicting the future.

In addition, it must be recognized that the prophets spoke to the people of their day in the language of their day. In most instances, the prophet's goal was to exhort the people to obey God's covenant. In the OT, the most common message of the prophets was to warn the people that if they failed to repent and obey the covenant, then God would bring about the curses

---

3. For a more complete discussion of the nature of prophecy, see chapter 5 of my *Understanding Eschatology: Why It Matters* (Eugene, OR: Wipf & Stock, 2013).

4. The word "prophecy" occurs seven times (surprised?) in the book of Revelation, always referring to the book itself (1:3; 11:6; 19:10; 22:7, 10, 18, 19).

5. Michael Gorman notes, "Prophecy, in the biblical tradition, is not exclusively or even primarily about making pronouncements and predictions concerning the future. Rather, prophecy is speaking words of comfort and/or challenge, on behalf of God, to the people of God in their concrete historical situation." Gorman, *Reading Revelation Responsibly: Uncivil Worship and Witness—Following the Lamb into the New Creation* (Eugene, OR: Wipf & Stock, 2011), 23. David deSilva adds, "Prophecy is essentially a 'word of the Lord' breaking into the situation of the Lord's people who need guidance or encouragement or a call to repentance and recommitment." David A. deSilva, *Unholy Allegiances: Heeding Revelation's Warning* (Peabody, MA: Hendrickson, 2013), 6.

of the covenant. At times, the prophets wrote to encourage the faithful with the knowledge that God will bring His promised blessings to them and soon defeat those who oppressed them.

For the most part, the prophets were not concerned with prognosticating, or telling the future, just for the sake of telling the future. They did make predictions; for example, they warned of coming judgment for the disobedient and they promised peace and prosperity for those who remain faithful. But the prophets did all of this not primarily to inform their audience of the future. Instead, their primary objective was to get the people of their day either to repent and be faithful or to remain faithful and know that God would soon relieve their suffering.

The prophets were primarily concerned with the actions of God's people in their present day. In some cases, the prophets' promises of blessings or threats of curses did not even come to fruition. This was because the people either failed to remain faithful and the promise of blessing was revoked or they repented and the threat of judgment was withdrawn.[6]

Isaiah, for example, addressed the people of his day who had strayed from the covenant by doing evil and neglecting justice (see Isa. 1:16–17). Isaiah aimed to bring them to repentance. The book of Isaiah opens with a clear summons to the people of Isaiah's day:

> "Wash yourselves, make yourselves clean;
> Remove the evil of your deeds from My sight.
> Cease to do evil,
> Learn to do good;
> Seek justice,
> Reprove the ruthless,
> Defend the orphan,
> Plead for the widow.

---

6. On this topic, note Jeremiah 18:7–10: "At one moment I might speak concerning a nation or concerning a kingdom to uproot, to pull down, or to destroy it; if that nation against which I have spoken turns from its evil, I will relent concerning the calamity I planned to bring on it. Or at another moment I might speak concerning a nation or concerning a kingdom to build up or to plant it; if it does evil in My sight by not obeying My voice, then I will think better of the good with which I had promised to bless it." This confirms that by its very nature prophecy was concerned with its original audience and their faithfulness to the covenant. If prophecy was by its very nature concerned with predicting the future, then any unfulfilled prophecies would be highly problematic.

Come now, and let us reason together,"
Says the LORD,
"Though your sins are as scarlet,
They will be as white as snow;
Though they are red like crimson,
They will be like wool.
If you consent and obey,
You will eat the best of the land;
But if you refuse and rebel,
You will be devoured by the sword." (Isa. 1:16–20)

This does not mean that Isaiah did not prophesy things that were ful-filled hundreds of years later. Indeed he did, as the rest of Scripture makes clear. What this does mean is that the focus of the message of Isaiah was upon the generation of his day. And what is true for the book of Isaiah is true for all the prophets: the prophets proclaimed a message first to the people of their own generations.

As a prophecy, then, John was not primarily concerned with predicting the future or telling when everything was to be fulfilled. Instead, John's readers and hearers would have discerned that he was speaking authorita-tively as the mouthpiece of God to them. This is why references to proph-ecy in the book of Revelation are linked to stern warnings such as "blessed is he who heeds the words of the prophecy of this book" (22:7; cf. 1:3; 22:18–19).

Finally, it is important to note that the language of the prophets often looks backward before it looks forward. For example, the prophets often referred to a future captivity of the people of God in terms of their earlier captivity in Egypt.[7] This corresponds with what we observed in chapter

---

7. This is very important for how one reads prophecy. Many popular writers on prophecy today propose that the biblical prophets were miraculously given insights into events of the distant future and were describing those events in the language of their day. They propose that only when we look at these events in light of their fulfillment (which is almost always considered to be the present day) are the words of the prophets and biblical writers able to be understood. This is famously argued by Hal Lindsey, who proposed that John was given a preview of twentieth century nuclear warfare, which he then described in the language of the first century (see Hal Lindsey, *There's a New World Coming* [Harvest House: Eugene, OR., 1984], 12–13). Lindsey suggests, "You might say that John was put into a 'divine time machine' and transported nineteen centuries into the future." The

4—namely, that the imagery for the book of Revelation is derived extensively from the OT.

Thus, while Scripture may be relevant to every generation, when it comes to the genre of prophecy and understanding the book of Revelation, it is essential to recognize that, as with an epistle, prophecy was intended to convey a message first of all to its original audience.

Apocalypse

The designation "apocalyptic" actually comes from the first word in the Greek text of the book of Revelation, *apokalypsis* ("revelation"). The word means "revelation" or "unveiling" and normally refers to a particular style of writing that flourished for several centuries prior to and up through the time of the writing of the book of Revelation.

It is this genre that usually causes the most consternation when it comes to understanding Revelation. But it need not. Though apocalypses might be known for their wild depictions of hybrid creatures with many heads, the reality is that apocalypses were used to convey several key principles.

First, and perhaps most significantly, apocalypses asserted that God was in control of history. This is one of the key features of the book of Revelation. John wrote to encourage his readers with the reality that Jesus has the keys of the kingdom (1:18), that Christ was dead and is alive forevermore (1:18), and that God will reward the faithful and judge the disobedient (20:4, 12–13). The simple matter is that apocalyptic language served as one of the best means to convey God's divine point of view. That is, apocalyptic simply asserts, from God's perspective, the way things really are. David deSilva notes:

> More than seeking to be *interpreted*, Revelation seeks to *interpret* the reality of the audience, showing them the true character of features of that landscape, identifying the true struggle that they must engage, naming the true stakes of choices before the hearers.[8]

---

problems with this thinking include the fact that, if this approach were true, the book of Revelation would have had little to no relevance to John's readers. For a response to the writings of Hal Lindsey see T. Boersma, *Is the Bible a Jigsaw Puzzle? An Evaluation of Hal Lindsey's Writings* (St. Catharines, Canada: Paideia Press), 1979.

8. David deSilva, *Seeing Things John's Way: The Rhetoric of the Book of Revelation* (Louisville: Westminster John Knox, 2009), 14. Emphasis original.

In addition, apocalypses were quick to point out that not only was God in control of history but also that history would unfold according to His plan. It is a mistake, however, to think that the apocalypses used symbolic language and numbers to secretly encode the exact times when everything will happen. The apocalypses were not concerned with detailing *when* it would all happen but that it *will* all happen. More importantly, apocalypses, like epistles and prophecies, were far more concerned with how the people of God responded to the message.

Of course, many of the apocalypses were convinced that the end would happen soon. They did not, however, intend to give precise details as to when the end of history would arrive. The book of Revelation also holds the conviction that it will take place soon: "The Revelation of Jesus Christ, which God gave Him to show to His bond-servants, the things which must soon take place" (1:1); "And he said to me, 'These words are faithful and true'; and the Lord, the God of the spirits of the prophets, sent His angel to show to His bond-servants the things which must soon take place" (22:6).

Why did the apocalypses tend to stress that it would all be over soon? Primarily to encourage their readers to persevere—hang in there, relief is coming soon![9] The book of Revelation contains this sense of imminence, not to contend that it will indeed actually be over soon as ordinarily understood, but in order to encourage a sense of urgency among the churches.

The book of Revelation, in fact, warns against any effort to determine when it will all end. After all, when the souls of those who were slain cry out and ask, "How long?" they are not given an answer as to when God will bring His vengeance—but only that God will do so:

> And there was given to each of them a white robe; and they were
> told that they should rest for a little while longer, until the number

---

9. The book of Revelation is likely using the notion of "soon" in terms of fulfillment. The "soon" of Revelation 1:1 and 22:6 may well be an allusion to Daniel 2:28, 29, and 45. If so, John might be arguing that the "soon" or "in the last days" of Daniel are now being fulfilled. That is, the "last days" of Daniel have begun. If this is so, then John is not making any statement as to how long it will be until the end (which fits very well with the fact that Revelation never gives any sort of details as to when the end will come), he is only saying that the period of the end has begun. See Beale, *The Book of Revelation: A Commentary on the Greek Text* (Grand Rapids: Eerdmans, 1999), 181–82.

of their fellow servants and their brethren who were to be killed even as they had been, would be completed also. (6:11)

The book of Revelation shows no interest in describing when it will all climax. Revelation, however, like other apocalypses, is deeply convinced that God will bring it all about.

Other features of apocalypses that are shared by the book of Revelation include the frequent use of repetition and recurring patterns, the use of highly figurative language, the symbolic use of numbers, and a dualistic view of reality (i.e., there are two kingdoms, two ages, etc.). I have already noted John's symbolic use of numbers. In chapters 10 and 11 we will examine John's dualistic understanding and his use of symbolism.

CONCLUSION

Our brief study of genres confirms that the nature of epistles, prophecies, and apocalypses are such that each was used to convey a message primarily to the people of the day. John was not writing in some secret code in order that some future generation might know "the signs of the times" and be able to predict the hour of Christ's return.[10]

The framing of the book of Revelation in an epistolary genre affirms that John was writing to the people of his day. At the same time, Revelation is a prophecy. As such, it presents us with the word of God to the people of the day—the prophetic word was relevant primarily to the people to whom the prophet spoke. Finally, even the use of the genre of apocalyptic does not separate the text from the people to whom John was writing.[11]

For Further Study

1. In light of the importance of numbers, why do you suppose there are seven churches in Revelation 2–3?
2. Read the seven letters of Revelation 2–3. Note that each letter has similar features. Make a chart and compare and contrast each of

---

10. On this, see Appendix 1.

11. Some may be initially uncomfortable with idea of Revelation being read as a prophecy or apocalypse containing so much symbolism, as it seems contrary to many popular ideas about the book. See Appendix 2 for discussion.

the letters. Which churches have no positive features? Which have nothing negative?

3. Read Revelation 11:1–6. Note that the two witnesses are said to prophesy (11:3, 6). In light of our understanding of prophecy and our understanding of the book of Revelation, what do you think is their message?

4. In light of our understanding at this point in our study, what do you think is the meaning of the "lake of fire" (19:20; 20:10, 14, 15; 21:8)?

5. Note that two of the seven churches in Revelation 2–3 have nothing negative written about them. What do you suppose that might mean for John's understanding of the condition of the church?

6. In this chapter, we have observed that John has used the genre of apocalyptic. Though I have not been able to detail in this introductory work all that this entails, it is worth noting here that one key element, common to many of the apocalypses, is that the writers were convinced that the last days had begun. For John, it appears that the last days were inaugurated with the coming of the Lamb (or the slaying of the Lamb). Compare the following translations from Daniel and the book of Revelation (note that the translations of the Daniel passages are the author's translations based on the Greek text of Daniel):

- Daniel 2:28: "What must happen in the last days"
- Daniel 2:29: "What must happen in the last days"
- Daniel 2:45: "The things which will be in the last days"
- Revelation 1:1: "What must happen quickly"
- Revelation 1:19: "What is about to happen after these things"
- Revelation 4:1: "What must happen after these things"
- Revelation 22:6: "What must happen quickly"

When we examine these passages in light of the fact that much of the apocalyptic imagery in Revelation derives from Daniel, what might we conclude about the relationship between Daniel and the book of Revelation? And what about John's understanding of Daniel's "last days"?

Application

1. The seven letters of Revelation 2–3 are written to exhort the people of God to maintain their witness in the world. There are several indications that one of the main threats to the churches was compromise with false teachings. A thorough study of the seven letters might reveal that some of the instances of compromise were a result of economic woes. What are some of the main threats of compromise that hinder the church today? Think about your local context, then consider the church in other parts of the world.

Conclusion to Part 2

I have been blessed to have taught the book of Revelation on numerous occasions in colleges, seminaries, and churches around the world. Over the course of these studies, the students come to see John was presenting Jesus as the fulfillment of the OT promises. I note carefully how John was encouraging his readers, and us today, to overcome. Quite regularly, someone, often with a sense of exasperation, will eventually interject, "Well if that is what John meant, then why didn't he just say it?"

The question makes perfect sense. Why use all the images and far-out language to say what Paul seems to say in a letter? A letter, after all, is less likely to be so confusing. The answer is simple. An apocalypse, with all of its vivid imagery, captures the mind, the heart, and the emotions. The images, like Jesus' parables, stick. We can all remember that Revelation is about a dragon chasing a woman and her offspring. Once we learn that the dragon is Satan and the woman, or at least her offspring, are the people of God, we can then realize that this is no game—Satan really is trying to devour God's people. We must overcome! Sure, this leaves open the possibility of misinterpretation. But that is no different from 1 Corinthians. All Scripture is subject to misinterpretation. In fact, all communication in general is subject to misinterpretation.

We have seen in this part of our study that John uses numbers to accent what he has said. In addition, we have learned that we must use caution when it comes to reading and understanding the book of Revelation. Because John has used genres that we, two thousand years later, are not well acquainted with, we must be careful.

In one sense, all of this means that our task of reading, understanding, and applying the book of Revelation is difficult. We must study and examine the nature of the language and the images in the book. For the average reader, this means that we must rely on trusted scholarly works.

At the same time, our task is not as difficult as some might want us to believe. After all, the best interpreters are children! Anyone can read and understand it, as long as we learn to let the language and imagery speak for itself. Trouble will come when we believe that we must decode everything. If we steer away from these dangers, then we can read and understand Revelation well: we must follow the Lamb.

PART 3

Reading Revelation as Literature

Introduction to Part 3

The book of Revelation is a stunning piece of literature. Its beauty is in its simplicity and its complexity. In its simplicity, as we learned in Part 1, the book of Revelation is about Jesus, and it is an exhortation to the people of God to overcome. In Part 2 we began to examine some of its complexity. We learned that Revelation uses numbers as a means to enhance the story. We also found that Revelation uses three genres that require some level of understanding in order to discern the nature of the language. In Part 3 we will examine the nature of John's narrative. The book of Revelation carries forth a story. Fortunately, as we will see, John provides his readers with plenty of clues that aid our understanding of the book.

Many contemporary readers of the book of Revelation are often so compelled to determine how everything in the book plays out in the real world that they look past John's verbal clues. These verbal clues are meant to convey a literary meaning more than an historical meaning. What I mean by this is that John's narrative must be read in light of the story that John is putting forth. This story has real-world implications: the people of God have a mission to fulfill. There really is an enemy of Christ and His people. As a result, there is a real-world struggle facing God's people, who must indeed overcome.

Reading Revelation as a story will help us discern John's message and its application for the people of God today. What we must be careful of is not to look past John's literary intent in our efforts to discern what the vision might mean in the contemporary world. For example, the book of Revelation says that the beast has ten heads (13:1). Some interpreters will immediately endeavor to determine what those ten heads might refer to—some have suggested the European Economic Community (EEC) or the European Union (EU).

The problem here is not simply the desire to decode. The problem is that we migrate to decoding too quickly. In doing so, we often lose sight of John's intent. When it comes to the beast, it appears that John is concerned that the beast is allied with the dragon and that it is waging war against the people of God (13:7). Such a realization should cause the readers great consternation. We should begin to meditate on how the beast might be waging war against God's people and how we might prepare for this battle.

Being overly consumed with identifying the beast may well cause the reader to lose sight of the very thing John wanted us to focus on: God's people have a real enemy whose goal is to destroy them. One of the serious flaws in decoding is that one tends to limit the meaning of the beast to the EEC or the EU. What if the ten heads represented the fullness of the nations that are aligned with the dragon and stand in opposition to God's people throughout history?

To limit the ten heads to one historical reality may mean ignoring the many occasions in history in which the beast has waged war against God's people—which ironically would be the very thing the dragon, who is the deceiver, wants (12:9). In other words, by focusing on decoding and attempting to determine how everything plays out in history, we may well have missed the fundamental meaning of the book of Revelation and, thereby, failed to discern how John's message is playing out in history!

Now I am not saying that we cannot decode at all. Instead, I am saying we cannot *begin* with decoding. We cannot allow our desire to decode impact our reading of the text too quickly. As I mentioned in the last part of our study, Revelation was written to affect our emotions. If our intellect is at the forefront, always trying to decode, then we lose some of the impact that Revelation was designed to have.

In addition, the book of Revelation appears to be far more concerned with giving a message than it is with how that message plays out in history. I do not mean to denigrate the importance of these matters and their playing themselves out in history; I simply mean that such questions are secondary. Consequently, once we are able to discern John's message, then we can begin to ask how such truths are being played out in history.

In this part of our study we will attempt to examine the structure of the book of Revelation. Our goal is to learn how to read and understand the book of Revelation in accordance with the manner in which John has arranged things. We will discern that John provides indicators, which a keen ear will pick up on (and I say "ear" because most of John's first "readers" would have actually been "hearers"—with one person reading the text and everyone else listening). These indicators aid us in discerning how the various passages relate to one another. We must remember that hearers cannot see chapter breaks, section breaks, or even paragraph breaks. A good ancient writer, then, had to structure his writing in such a way that hearers were able to discern such structural clues.

One of the primary manners in which ancient writers accomplished this was through the art of repetition. John repeats key words and phrases in order to assist the hearers in the flow of his narrative.

For example, the seven letters of the book of Revelation have a sort of structural repetition. Each letter begins with the customary "To the angel of the church in . . . write" (2:1, 8, 12, 18; 3:1, 7, 14). In addition, each of the letters ends with "he who has an ear, let him hear what the Spirit says to the churches" (2:7, 11, 17, 29; 3:6, 13, 22). In doing this, John helps his hearers by clearly marking the beginning and closing of each letter.

In Revelation 6, John describes the opening of the seven seals. At the opening of the first four seals, John maintains a fairy consistent introduction:

> Then I saw when the Lamb broke one of the seven seals, and I heard. . . . When He broke the second seal, I heard. . . . When He broke the third seal, I heard. . . . When the Lamb broke the fourth seal, I heard . . . (Rev. 6: 1, 3, 5, 7).

A first-century reader would indeed hear this repetition. There is a subtle intensification as the description of each seal is successively longer than the previous one. When John describes the opening of the fifth seal, this repetition is suddenly broken: "When the Lamb broke the fifth seal, I saw . . ." (6:9). Instead of hearing something, John now sees. This sudden change would have struck the ears of John's readers.

Over the next three chapters we will examine the book of Revelation in order to discern some of the clues John has provided us. In chapter 7 we will look at John's use of inclusios in order to discern some of the key messages of the book of Revelation.

In chapter 8 we will examine how John uses repetition to reveal how he has laid out his narrative. Though the structure of the book of Revelation is quite complex, we will observe that John provides key indicators that will guide us in determining the structure of the book.

In chapter 9 we will look at the fascinating manner in which John has woven his story. The story of the book of Revelation will frighten us, encourage us, and give us hope—all at the same time.

Of course, the nature of an introductory work such as this means that we will not attempt to venture into all the complexity of the structure of the book of Revelation. Instead, the aim here is to learn keys that will enable you to read and understand the book of Revelation more effectively.

CHAPTER 7

Inclusios: Structure and the Book of Revelation

In order to read the book of Revelation well we must learn to read it at the literary level. We must immerse ourselves in the story and refrain from attempting to discern how everything plays out in the real world. There will be a time and a place for that, of course. But to read the book of Revelation effectively one must remain in the literary world as long as possible.

UNDERSTANDING THE STORY

The book of Revelation certainly contains a story. One of the more difficult questions pertains to the nature of that story. In particular, how does the story unfold? For some, the narrative of the book of Revelation unfolds in a linear fashion: from point A to point B. Generally speaking, proponents of this view contend that the events described in Revelation chapter 6 are real-world events that take place before the events described in chapter 11, and so on.

For others, Revelation is circular, or recapitulatory. Proponents of this view agree that the story in the book of Revelation advances but they contend that it repeats itself. According to this view, the events depicted in the latter portions of the book of Revelation describe the same events that were depicted earlier. The latter events do so in a manner that adds depth or detail to the story.

Most views acknowledge that the narrative of the book of Revelation does move forward. After all, it ends with the return of Christ and the establishing of a new creation. Yet I will contend that the book of Revelation is not strictly linear. The issue is that there are several places in which the story appears to go backward. We can see that on several occasions it appears that the end has arrived, even though John does not actually narrate the return of Christ until chapter 19 and the descent of the new Jerusalem until chapters 21–22.[1]

For example, the cry of the nations following the breaking of the sixth seal appears to be heralding judgment day. They exclaim, "The great day of their wrath has come" (6:17). This would place the end in chapter 6.

Similarly, the blowing of the seventh trumpet appears to signal the return of Christ:

> Then the seventh angel sounded; and there were loud voices in heaven, saying, "The kingdom of the world has become the kingdom of our Lord and of His Christ; and He will reign forever and ever." (11:15)

That this event marks the return of Christ appears justified in light of the explicit statement that He has begun to reign and from the fact that the common threefold description of God ("who is and who was and who is to come"—1:8) now occurs in a twofold form:

> And the twenty-four elders, who sit on their thrones before God, fell on their faces and worshiped God, saying, "We give You thanks, O Lord God, the Almighty, who are and who were, because You have taken Your great power and have begun to reign." (11:16–17)

As noted earlier, the omission of "who is to come" in relation to God is quite striking. This fact is all the more remarkable in light of the fact that God is usually referred to with threefold titles. Are we to conclude that the omission of "who is to come" here is a result of the fact that He has already come? If this is so, then we have the end in chapter 11. What, then, do we

---

1. I fully realize the there are many debates as to what "the end" refers to in the book of Revelation. It is not necessary for us to engage in these debates in an introductory study such as this.

do with the descriptions of the second coming and the day of judgment in chapters 19 and 20?

It appears then that the book of Revelation both moves forward and it circles back. It is both linear and recapitulatory. Neither a linear nor a recapitulatory approach alone is sufficient—the structure of the book of Revelation is at the same time more simple and more complex than either of these two approaches (and their myriad proposals) are able to account for. We will focus on the simpler explanation in this study. As such, I do not intend to provide yet another detailed suggestion as to how the narrative of Revelation unfolds. The goal in this section is merely to introduce the reader to several keys that will enhance one's ability to interpret the book of Revelation. The reader will learn to discern John's clues as to how things are set forth in Revelation.

What I propose is that Revelation must be read first at the literary level. What I mean by this is that the twenty-first-century reader must constantly ward off modern questions as to how this all plays out in the real world. Whether this event happen before or after that event is not the type of question that John wants us to ask. This does not mean that such questions are not valid. Rather, it simply means that they need to wait for the proper time.

In order to read and understand the book of Revelation well we must first discern how the various parts of the book relate to one another. That is, how do they affect our reading of the story? We must ask if a given section expands on a previous section or if it is carrying the narrative forward.

REPETITIONS

At one level, discerning the nature of the narrative of Revelation is not as difficult as one might think. For John has provided us with clues that enhance our ability to discern how the various parts of the book of Revelation relate to one another. John does this by using the art of repetition.

Repetition was an important feature of ancient writing. Repetition allowed the hearer to recognize paragraph breaks, new sections, the relationship between sections, and even key structural clues to the nature of the whole book. This is such a central element to reading and understanding the book of Revelation that one could easily fill an entire book with examples. Instead, we will limit ourselves to an introductory look at some of the primary ones.

In the For Further Study section at the close of this chapter, the reader will be challenged to read and reread the book of Revelation in order to discern more of these connections.

INCLUSIOS

Ancient writings did not have chapter divisions, section headings, or paragraph breaks. Since these works were mostly read aloud, the presence of these things would have been of no use anyway. In order to help the readers/hearers follow along, ancient writers had to include verbal clues that would alert the readers/hearers of the beginning or close of a section.

A common technique for an ancient author was to open and close a section of a book, or even the whole work, by means of the repetition of a key phrase, idea, or image. That is, an author might bracket a paragraph, a story, a larger section, or even a whole book with such a repetition.

This literary device is called an inclusio. What we today accomplish by means of paragraph breaks, chapter breaks, and various section headings, an ancient author accomplished through inclusios.

John used a number of inclusios to frame the entire book of Revelation. That is, there are key phrases that appear at the beginning and at the end of the book of Revelation that serve to frame the entire book. The use of inclusios to frame an entire work is similar to what a modern writer does in telling us their purpose in the introduction and then reiterating what they have done in the conclusion. By observing these inclusios in the book of Revelation, we are able to discern in large measure some of John's primary objectives in writing.

For example, John opens and closes the book of Revelation with similar wording:

> The Revelation of Jesus Christ, which *God* gave Him *to show to His bond-servants, the things which must soon take place*; and He *sent* and communicated *it* by *His angel* to His bond-servant John (1:1, emphasis added). . . . And the Lord, the *God* of the spirits of the prophets, *sent His angel to show to His bond-servants the things which must soon take place.* (22:6, emphasis added)

From this inclusio we can see that the entire book of Revelation is a message from God Himself to John about what must soon take place.

Another example is found in 1:3 and 22:10. These verses frame the book of Revelation with "the time is near." As a result, we learn that, whatever the message of Revelation might be, we must act now. There is an urgency upon the people of God to listen and to act.

In 1:6 we see that John's introduction to the people of God affirms that they are "a kingdom, priests to His God and Father" (1:6). Then in Revelation 20 we see a group that is similarly described: "They will be priests of God and of Christ, and they will reign with Him for a thousand years" (20:6). The description in Revelation 1:6 reminds the readers of the charge to the OT people of God given to Moses after the Israelites had crossed the Red Sea. In Exodus 19 the Israelites were informed that God had rescued them for a purpose. They were to be "to Me a kingdom of priests and a holy nation" (Exod. 19:6).

This description at the opening of Revelation likely serves to connect the NT people of God and their mission in the book of Revelation with the promises of God to the Israelites. That this description recurs at the close of the book of Revelation, forming an inclusio with chapter 1, affirms that one of the central aims of the book of Revelation is to exhort the readers to fulfill their mission. God has made us "a kingdom, priests to His God and Father." Now get out there and accomplish the job!

Another inclusio that frames the entire book of Revelation occurs in the description of God "I am the Alpha and the Omega" (1:8; 21:6; 22:13). The importance of this inclusio is heightened when one realizes that Revelation 1:8 and 21:5–8 are the only two passages where the "One who sits on the throne" speaks. This is powerful. The Father only speaks from the throne at the beginning and the ending of the book. This alone should cause us to pause. His declaration is that He is the eternal source of all.

We also see that the book of Revelation opens and closes with reference to the seven churches: "John to the seven churches that are in Asia" (1:4) and "I, Jesus, have sent My angel to testify to you these things for the churches" (22:16). This inclusio reminds us that the people of God are the primary audience. This would begin with the seven churches of John's day and continue throughout history to us in the present.

Finally, the book of Revelation opens and closes with references to the book itself. In chapter 1 John is told that he must "write in a book what you see" (1:11). Then in chapter 22 the book of Revelation closes with an exhortation to do what the book says:

> I testify to everyone who hears the words of the prophecy of this book: if anyone adds to them, God will add to him the plagues which are written in this book; and if anyone takes away from the words of the book of this prophecy, God will take away his part from the tree of life and from the holy city, which are written in this book. (22:18–19)

The reference to the book at the beginning and the end, along with the fact that the closing passage parallels the opening by placing a great stress on hearing and doing what it says (cf. 1:3), suggests that the book of Revelation was written to encourage its readers to listen carefully and to be diligent to put it into practice.

CONCLUSION

The use of inclusios to frame the book of Revelation is an important feature. In order to interpret the book of Revelation well these inclusios must be noticed and pondered.

For Further Study

Over the next several chapters the focus of our For Further Study sections will be on the repetition of key terms and phrases. I am not asking for you to do a word study. A word study examines a word and its uses to discern its meaning. What I am suggesting here is to take the following key words and phrases and compare the passages in which they occur. The goal is to recognize how John uses the word or phrase throughout the book of Revelation (and not simply what the word means). This chapter will focus on words and phrases that frame the book or serve as additional inclusios.

1. Revelation is framed by reference to those who are "blessed" (1:3; 14:13; 16:15; 19:9; 20:6; 22:7, 14). Note that this word occurs seven times. How does this help us understand John's purpose for writing?
2. Revelation is framed by reference to "I am coming" (2:5, 16; 3:11; 16:15; 22:7, 12, 20). Note that this phrase also occurs seven times. What is the significance of this?
3. What is the significance of the fact that the warning about deception occurs near both the beginning and the end of Revelation?

Observe "leads astray/deceives": 2:20; 12:9; 13:14; 18:23; 19:20; 20:3, 8, 10. Note also the warnings about "lying" (14:5; 21:27; 22:15) and "liars" (2:2; 21:8). Read these passages and explain what the significance of these are for discerning the message of the book of Revelation.

4. There are a few other inclusios that occur in the opening and closing of the book of Revelation. Examine the following inclusios and see what their significance might be to the overall message of the book of Revelation:

   • The book of Revelation is mediated through angels (1:1; 22:6, 8, 16) and through John (1:1; 22:8). Note that the nature of apocalyptic writings is important here.
   • Revelation is rooted in God's word (1:2–3; 22:6–7, 9–10, 18–19).
   • Revelation is a prophetic word written down and communicated to churches (1:3; 22:6–7, 9–10, 18–19).

5. Examine John's use of "wilderness" in Revelation 12:6, 14. What is the possible significance of the fact that the woman in Revelation 12 fled into the wilderness? Do a study on the biblical use of wilderness (you might consult the *Dictionary of Biblical Imagery*). What events in Scripture occur in the wilderness? Do the prophets or the psalmists use wilderness with any special meanings? Now apply what you have learned to these instances of wilderness in the book of Revelation.[2]

Application

1. We have seen that, despite all the modern confusion about the book of Revelation, John has made his message clear to the careful reader. At this point in our study, what do you believe are John's key messages for his readers? Which stands out to you as the most significant?

---

2. Note that there is another use of wilderness later in the book of Revelation (17:3). We will postpone discussion on this until later.

CHAPTER 8

Repetition: Structure and the Book of Revelation

In the previous chapter I pointed out that John uses repetitions to form inclusios. That is, he repeats key phrases both at the beginning and the end of a section, a paragraph, or the whole book. This repetition serves as a frame and provides key indicators of John's intent in writing this book. As James Resseguie notes:

> The way John tells his story—the imagery, settings, metaphors, and so forth—is as important as what he has to say. How do bizarre creatures with traits of this world and the world below help the reader to understand the nature of evil? What is the significance of the hybrids of humans and beasts? How do the numerous threes, fours, sevens, and twelves form the construction material for John's story? What do the characters' clothing and accessories reveal about their inner traits? How is the master plot of a people longing for a homeland—exiled in Babylon, confined in Egypt, wandering in the wilderness, journeying to the promised land— worked out in the Apocalypse? Why are Babylon and Jerusalem portrayed as mirror opposites? These and other questions can be answered by paying close attention to the way John tells his story.[1]

---

1. James L. Resseguie, *The Revelation of John: A Narrative Commentary*, Kindle ed. (Grand Rapids: Baker, 2009), location 148.

In this chapter and the next, we will continue to observe repetitions in the book of Revelation. We will begin by observing John's use of repetitions as a means of connecting, to varying degrees, various narratives and sections within the book of Revelation.[2] In some cases, the connection is relatively apparent. For example, we find multiple references to a beast, a great multitude, the bride, the 144,000, and so on. It is quite reasonable to assume that the beast of chapter 11 is the same beast as that of chapter 13, which, in turn, is the same beast that is thrown into the lake of fire (19:20).

In other instances the connections are more difficult. For example, is the "little book" of Revelation 10 the same book as the one the Lamb takes from the Father in Revelation 5? This is more difficult because the language in each account is slightly different. The book is called a "little book" in Revelation 10:2, 9, 10; and is only referred to as a "book" (and not a "little book") in Revelation 5.

Even more intriguing are the instances in which repetitions are used in an intentionally contrastive manner. For example, both the Lamb in Revelation 5 and the beast in Revelation 13 are said to have been "slain" (Lamb in 5:6, 9, 12; 13:8; beast in 13:3).[3] Is this meant as an intentional contrast? The beast appears to look like Jesus, even though we know that it is not. That John intends for us to see a contrast is evident in that the second beast in Revelation 13 is said to have "two horns like a lamb" (13:11).

What are the readers intended to conclude from these contrasts? The answer, of course, is certainly a matter of interpretation. One proposal is that

---

2. Here is where a good translation is helpful to the average reader. Of course, consulting the Greek would be the ideal. But since this is not an option for many, the next choice would be to consult a good translation—or, even better, to compare several good translations. The goal is to discern when the book of Revelation is repeating itself. Sometimes context will influence a translator, however, to translate the same word appearing in two different contexts differently. These may well be good translations, but it may also be that John has repeated the same word or phrase in order for the hearer to recognize the connection with an earlier passage.

3. Some may contend that the beast in Revelation 13 is only said to appear "as if he was slain." This is where it is essential to consult the Greek. For in both in Revelation 5 and Revelation 13 the Greek uses the same wording. Note the NASB translates Revelation 5:6 with "as if slain" in reference to the Lamb. The reader should be able to discern that the Lamb didn't just look to have been slain, but he actually was. Otherwise we might be left puzzled as to whether or not the beast actually was slain or only appears to have been. The key is that the beast is described in a manner that suggests that many will associate him with Christ.

John was associating the beasts with Jesus in order to depict them as false Christs and false prophets. The NT warns us that false prophets will come in "sheep's clothing" (Matt. 7:15). Do we read the association of the beast with Christ in terms of this false association? Could it be that the following words of Jesus' serve as the background: "If anyone says to you, 'Behold, here is the Christ,' or 'There He is,' do not believe him" (Matt. 24:23)? Perhaps the beasts are satanic attempts to usurp the kingship of Christ.

This chapter will examine some of these connections. In the next chapter we will see how John uses repetition in order to carry along the narrative. The goal is to equip the reader to have a greater ability to discern the beauty and depth of the book of Revelation.

Before we begin, the reader of this book will be cautioned on several fronts. First, in order to discern that John is linking (or connecting in some way) two or more passages, we must be certain that the language is consistent in the Greek. This will leave most readers of this book with either a lot of homework or at the mercy of good scholarship. Second, just because John has connected two or more passages does not mean that his purpose for doing so is always readily apparent. The interpreter must be careful.

Finally, by way of clarification, I am not suggesting that Revelation has some deep-seated code that must be broken in order to discern the true meaning of the text. If someone advocates this, run—fast! What I am saying here is that John has provided us with more clues as to how the book is to be read.

REPETITION OF SOME KEY WORDS IN REVELATION

One of the best ways to see that John has carefully and intricately woven his work together is by examining his use of language and his repetition of key terms and phrases. In the remainder of this chapter we will examine a few examples in order to substantiate the point at hand. In the For Further Study section of this chapter, more examples will be provided that will allow readers to explore for themselves.

Diadems/Crowns

An example of John's use of repetition and its impact on how we read and understand the book of Revelation is his use of the term "diadem."[4] This

---

4. The NIV and NLT both translate this word as "crowns." Most of the translations

term, which refers to something that is worn by a ruler, occurs only three times in the book of Revelation.[5] Two of the uses appear close together (12:3; 13:1) and most readers will immediately recognize the repetition and the intended connection. The third use (19:12), however, occurs much later and its contrastive significance may well be missed by most.

The first occurrence of this term appears in Revelation 12:3 where the dragon is said to have "seven heads and ten horns, and on his heads were seven diadems." Of course, it might be somewhat striking to us that the dragon has diadems at all, though Satan is the "god of this world" (2 Cor. 4:4).

The narrative of Revelation 12 continues into the account of the first beast in Revelation 13. We are again taken aback by the fact that the beast also has diadems: "Then I saw a beast coming up out of the sea, having ten horns and seven heads, and on his horns were ten diadems" (13:1). That the dragon and the beast both have seven heads and ten horns likely serves to alert the reader that there is a strong connection between these two.[6] This connection is intensified by the fact that the beast, like the dragon, also has diadems. The beast, however, has ten diadems and he has them on his horns, while the dragon has seven diadems and he has them on his heads. We might be surprised to see seven, which throughout the book of Revelation has been used to signify completion, especially in regard to God; and ten, which is commonly associated in Scripture with completion or totality in relation to the law, used in relation to the dragon and the beast.

All of this serves to intensify the drama. Regardless of what the number of heads and horns and diadems might mean, the fact is clear: Things we expect to see in relation to God and Christ, we are seeing in relation to the dragon and the beast. From a literary perspective, we may note that the readers' emotions are stirred—whatever this means it is not good.

---

use "diadem." Translation is very important here in that it is important to distinguish this word from *stephanos*, which is customarily translated as "crown."

5. The Greek word here being discussed here is *diadēmata*, which may be translated as "crowns" or "diadems" and refers to that which is worn by a king or ruler. It is not the same word that is used in the description of the twenty-four elders who have "crowns" on their heads (4:4, 10), or of the woman clothed with the sun (12:1). The word used there is *stephanos* and refers to a victor's wreath (see also 2:10; 3:11; 6:2; 9:7; 12:1; 14:14).

6. The connection between the dragon and beast is quite deep. The dragon, in fact, is said to give to the beast "his power and his throne and great authority" (13:2).

The third occurrence of diadems provides the key. This time we see that it is Christ who has them: "His eyes are a flame of fire, and on His head are many diadems; and He has a name written on Him which no one knows except Himself" (19:12). That this description of Jesus is meant to contrast with the depiction of the dragon and the beast is apparent in the parallel language of the two accounts.[7] Like the dragon, Jesus has diadems on His head. Unlike both the dragon and the beast, however, each of which have a specific number of diadems (seven and ten), Jesus has "many." "How many?" we might ask. The specific number is not provided. We might conclude that "many" means more than the dragon and the beast, or even more than can be counted.

We might suspect that by the time the reader of the book of Revelation makes it to chapter 19 and sees Jesus with "many diadems" they are intended to conclude, "That's what I thought," or, "I knew it all along." The beast and the dragon are not really kings—Jesus is!

A look at the larger picture of Revelation serves only to confirm this. We know from the opening of the book of Revelation that Jesus is "the ruler of the kings of the earth" (1:5). We should have known all along that the dragon and his beastly rulers were false claimants to the throne.

John's message to the churches is clear: do not be deceived. Though the dragon and the beast appear to be enthroned in the present, and though the people of God are suffering under the rule of these evil creatures, the time will come when Jesus will be revealed as the true King of kings.

The use of diadems is a great example of the literary nature of the book of Revelation. A theme is introduced in the opening: Jesus is the king. Then we learn that false claimants are wearing diadems. Finally, the story climaxes in the revelation of Jesus in which He is crowned with *many* diadems.

To Gather Them Together for the War: Armageddon

One of the more debated topics in the book of Revelation is the war of Armageddon.[8] Though "Armageddon" only occurs in Revelation 16:16,

---

7. In addition to the use of "diadems," we should note that the beast has "blasphemous names" on his heads (13:1), while Jesus "has a name written on Him which no one knows except Himself" (19:12).

8. For a more complete discussion of Armageddon, see my *Understanding Eschatology*, chapter 11. See also Appendix 3.

there are three very similar references to "gathering" and "the war" (cf. 16:14; 19:19; 20:8).[9]

In looking at these passages we note first that the phrase "to gather them together for the war" appears in identical form in both Revelation 16:14 and 20:8. Revelation 20 expands on Revelation 16:14, 16:

> When the thousand years are completed, Satan will be released from his prison, and will come out to deceive the nations which are in the four corners of the earth, Gog and Magog, to gather them together for the war. (20:7–8)

In light of what we observed in chapter 7, it is possible that the identical nature of this phrase in 16:14 and 20:8 may well function as an inclusio. If so, it would have significant implications for how we read the book of Revelation.

It is important to note that this phrase also appears in 19:19, though this time it is not completely identical with the other two occurrences: "And I saw the beast and the kings of the earth and their armies assembled to make war against Him who sat on the horse and against His army." This description is very similar to the previous two references. The only difference is that Revelation 19:19 adds the verb "to make" and omits the pronoun "them." Though the language of Revelation 19:19 is not identical to that of Revelation 16:14 and 20:8, it is nonetheless very close—close enough, in fact, to suppose that the original readers would have likely connected the three passages.

There are additional reasons to suppose that John intended his original readers to connect the "war" in each of the three passages. First, we see that contextually the war in all three passages is universal. In both Revelation

---

9. The battle of Armageddon is a prime example of a place where contemporary readers move too quickly into asking questions pertaining to the nature of the depicted events. It is problematic and sometimes dangerous to wonder if this is a literal war. Those who assume that it is immediately begin to seek to know when and where. The book of Revelation, however, is not concerned with such questions. This doesn't mean that we cannot ask them; rather, it simply means that these should not be our primary questions. What the book of Revelation is depicting may or may not necessarily correspond to particular events. Revelation is less concerned with wars that are fought with weapons between the nations, than with wars waged by the dragon and his minions against the people of God.

16:14 and 19:19, the war is waged by the "kings" of the whole world. That the war is also universal in Revelation 20:8 is clear in that it includes "the nations which are in the four corners of the earth." The reference to the "four corners of the earth" affirms the universal nature of this war (recall from chap. 5 that four is commonly used in connection to the fullness of creation).

That these references to the war are depicting the same war is also confirmed by the fact that the wars are waged by the kings in both Revelation 16:14 and 19:19. Though Revelation 20:8 does not mention kings, it does mention Gog and Magog, which represent pagan nations that oppose the people of God.[10]

In addition, in each instance the war appears to be waged against Christ and His followers. Revelation 19:19 states explicitly that the war is waged "against Him who sat on the horse and against His army." Similarly, Revelation 20:9 tells us that those who wage the war against Christ in 20:8 "surrounded the camp of the saints and the beloved city." Though the war in Revelation 16:14, 16 is not explicitly declared to be waged against Christ and the people of God, there are good reasons to suspect that this is indeed the case. Most notable is the exhortation sandwiched within the description of the war in 16:14, 16. Here in Revelation 16:15, the people of God are warned to "stay awake." That they are to "stay awake," or "be prepared," suggests that this war has some effect on the people of God.

If these three accounts are depicting the same war, then we must ask why John did not simply use the exact same expression in all three passages. The answer may well reside with what we have already come to learn, namely, that when John repeats phrases verbatim they seem to have a structural significance.[11] That is, John uses verbatim repetition to mark the beginning and end of sections, or to form an inclusio. In this instance, the verbatim repetition of Revelation 16:14 and 20:8 forms an inclusio. If John had used the identical phrase in Revelation 19:19, which is the middle of Revelation 16:14–20:8, it could well have signaled an end to the discussion of the war and broken up the larger section.

---

10. Cf. Ezekiel 38:2 for the only other mention of Gog and Magog together. Gog is mentioned in Ezekiel 38:3, 14, 16, 18; 39:1, 11. Reference to Magog is found in Genesis 10:2; 1 Chronicles 1:5; Ezekiel 39:6.

11. This is argued at length by Richard Bauckham, *Climax of Prophecy* (Edinburgh: T&T Clark, 2000), chapter 1.

WHAT DOES ALL THIS MEAN?
A LITERARY PERSPECTIVE

The links between the three depictions of gathering for the war are strong. The first and second occurrences (16:14; 19:9) are connected by the fact that the war is waged by the kings of the earth. The first and third occurrences (16:14; 20:8) are unquestionably linked by the use of the identical expression "to gather them together for the war." The second and third occurrences (19:19; 20:8–9) are connected by the fact that the war is explicitly said to be waged against Christ and His people. There is no way around it. From a literary perspective there is no doubt that John, by means of repetition and the use of other verbal connections, intends for his readers to read these three passages in light of one another.

This conclusion has significant implications for how we read the book of Revelation. If we believe that Revelation unfolds in a linear fashion, then we are forced to conclude that these three passages cannot refer to the same event. After all, the war in Revelation 16:14, 16 occurs before the pouring out of the seventh bowl (16:17–21), which signals the return of Christ. The war in Revelation 19:19, however, follows (or is an event at the time of) the return of Christ in 19:11–16, which occurs after the outpouring of the seventh bowl. And the war in Revelation 20:8 follows the thousand years of 20:4–7, which in most linear readings occurs after the return of Christ.

But what if Revelation is not intending to provide us with such a purely linear way of thinking? After all, a linear way of looking at history and the world is very much part of a Western mindset. The ancient world was not as deeply rooted in a linear way of thinking. What if John was more concerned with providing a narrative that built to a climax?

This is very hard for modern Westerners, as well as those who have been influenced by modern Western thinking. We are so concerned with what the text means and with how this all plays out in history that we have difficulty grasping what John is setting forth. We assume that John is in some sense writing history or prophetic history. As a result, we assume that "the war" in each of these three passages cannot be the same, because the chronological contexts in which they take place differ.

The problem with reading the book of Revelation with these assumptions is that we overlook some significant features of John's writing. However, if we look at the war in these three passages from a literary perspective, as John seems to have intended for us to do, then we might conclude the following:

First, from the account in Revelation 16, we see that the war is waged by Satan and his demonic hordes:[12]

> And I saw coming out of the mouth of the dragon and out of the mouth of the beast and out of the mouth of the false prophet, three unclean spirits like frogs; for they are spirits of demons, performing signs, which go out to the kings of the whole world, to gather them together for the war of the great day of God, the Almighty. (16:13–14)

In addition, the parenthetical exhortation warns us that this war calls for perseverance on the part of the people of God: "Behold, I am coming like a thief. Blessed is the one who stays awake and keeps his clothes, so that he will not walk about naked and men will not see his shame" (16:15). At this point, things are not looking good for the people of God. It looks like a horrific war that we must endure.

The description in Revelation 19 helps the people of God put this war in a better light. For here the war is associated with the return of Christ. The stage is set as Christ is coming on a white horse, which depicts him as a warrior-king.[13] On His return, "the armies which are in heaven, clothed in fine linen, white and clean, were following Him on white horses" (19:14).

The primary focus of the war in Revelation 20 is that Satan will suffer the same fate as the beast and the false prophet: "And the devil who deceived them was thrown into the lake of fire and brimstone, where the beast and the false prophet are also; and they will be tormented day and night forever and ever" (20:10).

What do we do, then, with the fact that Revelation 19 seemingly places the war at the time of Christ's return, while the war in Revelation 20 occurs after the thousand years? This is a difficult question to address. From a literary perspective the answer appears to be that John simply intended to describe God's justice on the beast and the false prophet (Revelation 19)

---

12. That the war is the work of Satan is made explicit by John in Revelation 12–13.

13. See chapter 12 for a more complete discussion of holy war in the book of Revelation.

separately from that of the dragon/Satan (Revelation 20). That is, the two accounts are separated in order to give greater emphasis to the judgment: first, to the beasts; and then, second, to Satan.

Revelation 20, then, in narrating the judgment of Satan, places the war after the release of Satan from his prison (cf. 20:7). From a literary perspective, Revelation 20 confirms that the war is the work of Satan: he goes out to "deceive the nations which are in the four corners of the earth, Gog and Magog, to gather them together for the war" (20:8). Since it would be illogical to have Satan as the mastermind of the war when he is still bound, John narrates that Satan is released.

So, what do we do with all this? We prepare for war!

CONCLUSION

We have learned that an important consideration for reading, understanding, and applying the book of Revelation is to determine the literary features with which John has constructed his work. Foremost among them is John's use of repetition. We learned in chapter 7 that John uses inclusios to frame the overall message of his book. In this chapter we have seen that John uses repetition to link sections.

For Further Study

It appears that John uses repetition to connect various accounts. He uses verbatim repetition of longer phrases to indicate structural markers (i.e., section breaks). For the questions below, pay attention to the examples of repeated words and phrases in Revelation. Note again that I am not asking you to do a word study. What I suggest you to do here, instead, is to take the key words and phrases listed below and compare the passages in which they occur: How does John use this word or phrase throughout the book of Revelation? How does this impact our understanding of the book of Revelation?

1. What is the significance of "witness" in the book of Revelation? (see 1:5; 2:13; 3:14; 11:3; 17:6).
2. Observe that the description of the ministry of the two witnesses begins and ends by describing them as "prophesying" (11:3, 6). What does this say about their role? Does this help identify who they are or represent (see question 5 below)?

3. Note the repetition of "perseverance" (1:9; 2:2, 3, 19; 3:10; 13:10; 14:12). What does this add to our understanding of the book of Revelation?

4. Compare and contrast the references to *stephanos* ("crowns"—2:10; 3:11; 4:4, 10; 6:2; 9:7; 12:1 14:14). What might be the significance of this for our understanding of the book of Revelation?

5. The word "lampstand" occurs in the following passages: 1:12, 13, 20 (twice); 2:1, 5; 11:4. What is the significance of the fact that the two witnesses are called lampstands? How does this help us discern who/what the two witnesses are?

6. Many suggest that the word "sign," which occurs seven times from 12:1–19:20, is a structural marker. But it appears that John uses longer phrases identically in order to delineate structure. Examine the seven occurrences of "sign" in Revelation and discern their importance: 12:1, 3; 13:13, 14; 15:1; 16:14; 19:20.

7. The phrase "many waters" is striking. In 1:15 is it used of Christ's voice. Note the other references to "many waters" (14:2; 17:1; 19:6). Observe that in 14:2 and 19:6 "many waters" is closely linked to a great multitude, and that in 17:15 the "many waters" on which the harlot sits are said to be "peoples and multitudes and nations and tongues." What is the significance of this?

8. Examine the following examples of the words "was given" (*edothē*): 6:2, 4 (twice), 8, 11; 7:2; 8:2, 3; 9:1, 3, 5; 11:1, 2; 13:5 (twice), 7 (twice), 14, 15; 16:8; 19:8; 20:4. Note that this word is commonly (if not universally) used by John as a divine passive (i.e., God is the agent). How does this help us understand another of John's purposes for writing?

9. The bodies (lit. "body" in Greek) of the two witnesses are said to lie in the street of "the great city" (11:8). The phrase "the great city" also occurs in 16:19; 17:18; 18:10, 16, 18, 19, 21. Does this help us identify the "great city" in 11:8? Note that the difficulty is that the "great city" in chapters 17–18, called "Babylon," appears to represent Rome, but the "great city" in 11:8 is said to be "where also their Lord was crucified."

10. A person's name had great importance in the first century. Examine the use of "name" in the book of Revelation: "the name of My God," "the name of the city of My God," "My new name" (3:12; cf.

14:1; 22:4); "fear Your name" (11:18); "on his heads were blasphemous names" (13:1); "to blaspheme His name" (13:6); "the name of the beast or the number of his name" (13:17); "the mark of his name" (14:11); "the number of his name" (15:2); "full of blasphemous names . . . and on her forehead a name was written" (17:3, 5); "He has a name written on Him which no one knows except Himself. . . . His name is called The Word of God. . . . And on His robe and on His thigh He has a name written" (19:12, 13, 16). Note especially the use of "name" in 13:1, 6, 17; 14:11, and its apparent contrast with 14:1. What might be the significance for discerning the mark of the beast and the seal of God?

Application

1. From these brief examples of John's use of repetition, we learn that the message for the people of God is to stand firm. Jesus is the true King. And though the dragon and his minions are waging war against Christ and against His people, his efforts will come to an end at the return of Christ. At that time—whatever that may mean for us in the real world is beside the point—the beast, the false prophet, and Satan himself will all be judged. Then those who have overcome will be resurrected. And "blessed and holy is the one who has a part in the first resurrection; over these the second death has no power" (20:6). What difference does understanding all of this make for you?

CHAPTER 9

Reading Revelation as a Story

It is not uncommon for introductory studies of the book of Revelation to discuss at length the literary nature of the book of Revelation. As mentioned above, some suggest that the book of Revelation describes actual events that take place in a linear fashion over time, while others propose that Revelation is recapitulatory—that is, that the narrative in Revelation repeats itself, perhaps giving further details or clarifications as it proceeds. Many of these proposals are quite sophisticated and often lend to more confusion. The sheer presence of so many conflicting ideas suggests that perhaps no one explanation will suffice.

It is my proposal that the book of Revelation presents a story that is moving toward a climax. Granted, it is a complex story—sometimes moving forward and at other times moving backward. Nonetheless, there is a clear storyline. Discerning the key elements of this story is an important step toward understanding the book of Revelation.

Because this is an introductory work, we will not attempt to determine all the subtleties of Revelation's narrative. Our primary concern will be to demonstrate that it is indeed carrying a story forward. To do so, we will only examine one key element of this story and its corollary, namely, that the narrative of Revelation sets forth God's answer to the prayers of the saints and His concern for the redemption of the nations.

THE PRAYERS OF THE SAINTS AS A KEY TO UNDER-STANDING THE NARRATIVE OF REVELATION

Revelation chapter 1 opens with an introduction that lays the foundation for all that follows. As I noted in the previous two chapters, several key phrases frame the entire book and provide us with insights pertaining to John's objectives. Chapters 2 and 3 of the book of Revelation contain seven letters to seven churches in the Roman province of Asia Minor. These addresses were written to seven real churches at the time John penned the book of Revelation.

The setting for the main narrative in the book of Revelation, then, begins in chapter 4 with John being taken into heaven. John sees the Father sitting on a throne and surrounded by creatures who worship Him "day and night" (4:8). We learn that the Father is the sovereign creator of all things and because of this He receives worship (4:8–11).

In Revelation 5, John sees a scroll in the Father's right hand. This scroll is sealed closed with seven seals. John becomes distraught because no one was found worthy to open the scroll (5:1–3). Amidst John's angst, he *hears* that the Lion "has overcome" and is worthy to open the scroll (5:5–6). He then looks and *sees* a Lamb that was slain (5:6). The Lamb proceeds to take the scroll from the right hand of the Father (5:7). John then sees four living creatures and twenty-four elders, who have golden bowls full of incense. The incense, we are told, is "the prayers of the saints" (5:8). The four living creatures and the twenty-four elders fall down and worship the Lamb because He is worthy to open the scroll (5:8-9). And they sing "a new song" (5:9).

The narrative continues in chapter 6, where the Lamb begins to open the scroll by breaking one seal at a time. When the Lamb breaks the fifth seal we are introduced to "the souls of those who had been slain," who are under the altar crying out to God for vengeance: "And they cried out with a loud voice, saying, 'How long, O Lord, holy and true, will You refrain from judging and avenging our blood on those who dwell on the earth?'" (6:10). This group of souls is composed of martyrs—those who died in the cause of the gospel. They are told "that they should rest for a little while longer, until the number of their fellow servants and their brethren who were to be killed even as they had been, would be completed also" (6:11).

It is here that we might begin to wonder if the cry of the souls for vengeance (6:10) is the same as the prayers of the saints (5:8). That is, do the golden bowls full of incense, which represent the prayers of the saints, correspond to the cry for justice/vengeance on the part of the martyrs? At this point of the narrative, we certainly do not know—and we have no express indication to presume that this is the case.

This supposition, however, gains credibility in the opening of chapter 8. John sees another angel come and stand before the altar (8:3). John then observes that this angel has a golden censor and much incense was given to him,

> so that he might add it to the prayers of all the saints on the golden altar which was before the throne. And the smoke of the incense, with the prayers of the saints, went up before God out of the angel's hand. (8:3–4)

Here again, John connects incense to the prayers of the saints.

A careful reading of Revelation reveals several indications that the prayers offered upon the altar in Revelation 8 are to be viewed in light of the prayers of the saints contained in the bowls of the four living creatures and the twenty-four elders in Revelation 5, as well as the cries of the martyrs in Revelation 6. Among such indications is the fact that both Revelation 5 and 8 refer to incense, and this incense is associated with the prayers of the saints (5:8; 8:3–4). Furthermore, that the angel in Revelation 8 stands before the altar also links the prayers of the saints to the cry of the martyrs. After all, this angel appears to be standing before the altar from which the martyrs are crying out (6:9).

It is at this point that we may begin to see traces of the narrative that is being woven into the fabric of Revelation. Could it be that John wants us to see that the prayers of the saints (which may correspond to the martyrs' cry for vengeance) have gone up before God and are being answered because the Lamb has overcome and is worthy to open the scroll? If this is so, then we might propose that one of the narrative concerns of Revelation is to depict God's response to the prayer of the saints. As the reader proceeds through the book of Revelation, this conjecture gains in credibility.

THE REDEMPTION OF THE NATIONS

Before continuing to examine the book of Revelation in light of God's answer to the prayers of the saints, it is important to digress for a moment. Many contemporary readers may have trouble with the notion that one of the primary storylines in the book of Revelation is concerned with God's reply to His people's plea for vengeance—even if we understand vengeance in terms of justice here.

What is important to grasp (and we would be remiss if we overlooked this) is that God's vengeance is not exclusive of His desire to bring redemption, or salvation, to the nations. In fact, the redemption of the nations is a primary, and perhaps an even more important, theme than that of God's response to the prayers of the saints. This is evident in that the primary depiction of the people of God in the book of Revelation is in terms of their role as God's witnesses. This is why, as I have noted, they are depicted as lampstands.

Thus, in addition to the storyline of God's answering the prayers of the saints, the book of Revelation sets forth the fulfillment of God's promise to bring redemption to the nations. This can be seen from the fact that the conclusion to the book of Revelation includes this description of the new Jerusalem: "The nations will walk by its light, and the kings of the earth will bring their glory into it. . . . [A]nd they will bring the glory and the honor of the nations into it" (21:24, 26).

That the salvation of the nations is an important element in the story of Revelation is also evidenced by the fact that when the Lamb takes the scroll from the Father, the living creatures and the elders proclaim:

> Worthy are You to take the book and to break its seals; for You were slain, and purchased for God with Your blood men from every tribe and tongue and people and nation. You have made them to be a kingdom and priests to our God; and they will reign upon the earth. (5:9–10)

Corresponding to this, we learned in the opening of our study that the people of God are called to overcome as faithful witnesses by imitating Jesus—the One who is the "faithful witness" (1:5) *par excellence*, and the One who has Himself overcome (3:21). This brings us back to the response to the martyrs' plea in Revelation 6. They were told that the Lord would not grant vengeance for them "until the number of their fellow servants and their brethren who were to be killed even as they had been, would be completed also" (6:11).

Here also we may detect a basis for recognizing a concern for the salvation of the nations in God's reply to the prayers of the martyrs. This is apparent in that the response to their plea is to wait because not all those who are going to suffer and die for the kingdom have been killed (6:11).

Underlying the book of Revelation is the notion that the means by which God redeems the nations is through the persevering, faithful witness of the people of God—a witness that may well end in their deaths. To say, then, that they must wait for the rest to be killed for the gospel, may well be the same as saying that they must wait for the nations to be redeemed.

If we put together these two storylines—the martyrs' request for vengeance and God's desire to bring redemption to the nations—we are driven to ask if the reason for the delay in the response to the martyrs' request for vengeance is related to God's desire to redeem the nations. If this is so (and I believe that it is) then we might conclude that there is a delay in answering the martyrs' prayers so that, in fact, the nations might be redeemed.[1]

GOD'S ANSWER TO THE PRAYERS OF THE SAINTS

I have suggested that one of concerns in the opening of Revelation's narrative was God's answer to the prayers of the saints for vengeance (6:9–11). When we turn to the close of the book of Revelation, we observe that, indeed, it is their prayers that have been answered.

Revelation 17 and 18 narrate the judgment of the harlot Babylon and the laments of her accomplices. This woman—whomever or whatever she may represent is not essential at this point—is described as follows: "And I saw the woman drunk with the blood of the saints, and with the blood of the witnesses of Jesus" (17:6). The harlot, then, is depicted as one who has shed the blood of God's people.

The narrative of Revelation 17 and 18 makes it clear that God's judgment on the harlot is due to the fact that she has killed the people of God. Revelation 18 announces the judgment of the harlot Babylon: "Fallen, fallen is Babylon the great!" (18:2). The account of her destruction climaxes with John's exhortation to the people of God: "Rejoice over her, O heaven, and you saints and apostles and prophets, because God has pronounced judgment for you against her" (18:20). The text is clear: God's judgment of the harlot is directly related to her persecution of God's people.

This thought is further reiterated in Revelation 19. Here we learn of a great multitude that shouts, "Hallelujah! Salvation and glory and power

---

1. This point is argued further in my *Understanding Eschatology: Why It Matters* (Eugene, OR: Wipf & Stock, 2013), chapter 9.

belong to our God" (19:1).[2] This great multitude rejoices over the destruction of the harlot. In doing so, they exclaim, "He has avenged the blood of His bond-servants on her" (19:2). Thus the judgment of the great harlot brings relief to the people of God and an answer to their prayers. The cry "when are you going to avenge our blood?" (paraphrase of 6:10) has been heard. Therefore, God's people rejoice!

When we turn to Revelation 20, we find further evidence that the narrative of Revelation has been concerned with the prayers of the martyrs all along. John notes that he saw

> the souls of those who had been beheaded because of their testimony of Jesus and because of the word of God, and those who had not worshiped the beast or his image, and had not received the mark on their forehead and on their hand; and they came to life and reigned with Christ for a thousand years. (20:4)

Are these the same as the martyrs in Revelation 6:9–11 who cried out for vengeance? That they are is suggested by the fact that both groups are killed because of "the word of God" and because of "their testimony" (6:9; 20:4).[3] Though the understanding of Revelation 20 is highly debated and beyond the scope of our study, it is important to note that Revelation 20 appears to provide the conclusion to the fate of the souls under God's altar: they come to life (20:4).

That John intends us to link the account of the cry of the martyrs (6:10) and the rejoicing of the great multitude (19:2) is further confirmed by the use of the word "avenge" in both 6:10 and 19:2. In the book of Revelation, this word is only found in these two verses. In addition, both occurrences are further linked by the fact that the word "avenge" is associated with "blood." In Revelation 6, the martyrs asked how long God was going to refrain from "avenging our blood" (6:10). In Revelation 19, the great multitude rejoice because God "has avenged the blood of His bond-servants on her" (19:2).

---

2. This great multitude is likely the same group that was introduced in Revelation 7. This is important to the overall story of the book of Revelation.

3. The only differences between the two passages, which are not significant enough to counter the argument, are the order of the words and the fact that 6:9 says "the testimony," while 20:4 adds "the testimony of Jesus."

Furthermore, the blood that is avenged, and for which the great multitude rejoices, is that of God's "bond-servants" (19:2). The reference to bond-servants further associates this account with the cry of the martyrs in Revelation 6. There the martyrs had asked God when He would "avenge our blood" (6:10). The martyrs were then told that they "should rest for a little while longer, until the number of their fellow servants and their brethren who were to be killed even as they had been, would be completed also" (6:11). The word *syndouloi*, translated by the NASB as "fellow servants" (6:11), derives from the same root as the word *douloi*, a form of which is translated "bond-servants" in Revelation 19.[4] This further links the two accounts.

CONCLUSION

It indeed appears to be the case that the book of Revelation has a storyline. The story begins in Revelation 4 and 5. Here we learn that the Lamb is worthy to open the scroll and to receive the same worship as the Father.[5] And we are introduced to the four living creatures and the twenty-four elders who have the prayers of the saints (5:8). The story continues as the martyrs cry out of vengeance (6:9–11). And though the martyrs are told that they must wait a little longer, we find that as early as chapter 8 the answer to the prayers of the saints is already set in motion. Their prayers are lifted up to God (8:4). It is not until we reach the judgment of the harlot (Revelation 17–18) and the rejoicing of the great multitude (Revelation 19) that we find confirmation that the prayers of the martyrs have been answered.

That it is the prayers of the martyrs that are answered can be seen from the fact that the word "avenge" occurs only twice in the book of Revelation, that both occurrences are associated with blood, and that the blood is that of God's "fellow servants/bond-servants" (6:10; 19:2). It appears, then, that the prayers of the saints in Revelation 6:10 are indeed one of the key elements of the narrative of the book of Revelation.

Though to be thorough we would need to survey the book of Revelation

---

4. The difference between "bond-servants" in 19:2 and "fellow servants" in 6:11 is that the preposition syn (commonly meaning "with") is affixed to the word douloi in 6:11, resulting in the translation "fellow-servant."

5. See question 6 in the For Further Study section of chapter 1.

in much more detail than we have done here, it appears at this point that one of primary features of the narrative of the book of Revelation is God's concern to bring justice to His people. This justice, of course, is not independent of God's mercy and His desire to bring redemption to the nations; in fact, it is God's desire to save the nations that appears to be the cause of the delay in God's answer to the prayers of the saints.

If we were to continue this exploration, and to some extent the For Further Study questions will allow the readers to do so, we would see that it is through the faithful witnessing to the "word of God" and "the testimony of Jesus," for which the people of God are killed, that the nations are saved.

For Further Study

We have seen that Revelation weaves a story around key themes. The following exercises are not meant to suggest that each of the terms and phrases are at the same level of importance as such themes. Nonetheless, it does appear that certain terms and phrases progress throughout the course of the book of Revelation. Observing how John uses such expressions throughout the book of Revelation may well help us discern John's meaning more deeply.

1. What do you think is the importance of John's exhortation to the people of God to keep their clothes with them lest they be naked and ashamed (16:15)?

2. Clothes appear to have a significant role in the book of Revelation. Revelation describes angels (or angel-like creatures) as clothed, and further describes the clothes of the harlot and the great city. Sometimes Revelation identifies what they are or will be clothed with: for example, a long robe, white robes, a cloud, sackcloth, the sun, pure bright linen, fine linen, a robe dipped in blood, and so on. Note that "fine linen" is also mentioned as a commodity available in the great city (18:12). Revelation urges the people of God to clothe themselves, warns them that some have soiled their clothes, promises that God will clothe them, and describes the people of God in heaven as those who are clothed. Carefully compare and contrast the following passages:

- Jesus and the people of God "clothed": *endyō* (1:13; 15:6; 19:14); *periballō* (3:5, 18; 7:9, 13; 11:3; 19:8, 13).[6]
- Clothing for others: twenty-four elders (4:4); angels (10:1; 15:6); the woman (12:1); the harlot (17:4; 18:16).

3. What is the significance of clothing? Why is so much attention given to it? What was John trying to convey to his readers/hearers?
4. Is there a significance to the similarity between the clothing of the people of God and the clothing of Christ? If so, what is it?
5. Is there a significance to the clothing of the harlot? If so, what is it?
6. Examine "stand(ing)" in the following passages: 3:20; 5:6; 8:2, 3; 10:5, 8; 11:4, 11; 12:4, 18; 14:1; 15:2. What does this say about "standing"?
7. Note the shift that occurs in the closing occurrences of "stand": 18:10, 15, 17; 19:17; 20:12. In light of all the above, assess the book of Revelation's notion of "stand(ing)."
8. What do you suppose is John's answer to the question, "Who is able to stand?" (6:17). Hint: note 7:1, 9.
9. In Revelation 5 the Lamb takes the book that is in the Father's hand (5:1–10). In chapters 6–8 the book is then opened. In chapter 10, we find a strong angel having in his hand "a little book" (it is called "little book" in 10:2, 9, 10; and "book" in 10:8), which was open. Considering the notion that Revelation is presenting a narrative, what might this mean for identifying the books in the passages above? Is this the same book? Why or why not?
10. If Revelation is presenting a narrative, then what might this mean for the narrative of the two witnesses? Note that John is told to prophesy (10:11) and then proceeds to perform a prophetic act of measuring (11:1–2). What might this mean for determining the identity of the two witnesses and the duration of their ministry? In other words, are they two individuals that live (or have lived) at some point in history and ministered for a period of time— perhaps a literal three-and-one-half years? Or do they represent a corporate entity whose prophetic work transcends a single point in time?

---

6. Be cautious about making grand assertions based on the use of different Greek words. Sometimes authors vary their terms because it makes for better writing.

Application

1. In light of Revelation's story—that God is answering the prayers of the saints—what do you suppose is the message(s) of the book of Revelation for the people of God then and now?
2. What do you suspect is your role in this story?
3. What will you commit to do as a result of this?

Conclusion to Part 3

The book of Revelation is a masterpiece of literature. Revelation narrates a story that is complex, yet not too elusive. John has left us plenty of insights to aid us as we endeavor to discern its story.

One of John's strategies has been to repeat key terms and phrases to form inclusios. In a number of instances these inclusios frame the entire book of Revelation and provide insight into John's purpose for writing. Thus we learn that the book of Revelation was written "to show His bond-servants what must soon take place" (1:1; 22:6), and to encourage its readers both that they are kings and priests (1:6; 20:6) and that they can trust what they have read because its source is the eternal "Alpha and Omega" (1:8; 21:6; 22:13).

John also repeats key phrases to form inclusios that frame sections within the book. Recognizing these helps provide insights into the nature of the narrative of Revelation.

In addition, John's use of repetition has allowed us to see connections that we might not have otherwise recognized. The repetition of the phrase "gathered them together for the war" (16:14, 16; 20:8–9; cf. 19:19) led us to conclude that Revelation 16:14, 16; 19:19; and 20:8 should be read in light of one another. The result is that we see that the nations of the world are at war against Christ and the people of God. And God's people must "stay awake."

Finally, we have seen that there is a narrative thread to the book of Revelation. In the midst of it all, there is a story that is being played out, a story that appears to move both forward and backward. One key element of this story is that God's people have called for vengeance and He has heard their cry.

PART 4

Issues and Themes in the Book of Revelation

Introduction to Part 4

In this final part of our study we will continue our investigation into how to read, understand, and apply the book of Revelation by addressing some additional themes and issues.

First, I will address the presence of dualism. In short, dualism presupposes that there are two opposed or contrasting realms. The dualism of the book of Revelation primarily manifests itself in terms of the contrasts both between the dragon/beast(s) and Christ (or the parody of the latter by the former) and between those who follow the beast and the followers of the Lamb. Chapter 10 will explore this topic.

Chapter 11 will then examine the issue of the symbolism of the book of Revelation. I have saved the discussion of symbolism to this point for a simple reason: It was important to have the foundation that we have laid for understanding Revelation before we could broach this subject. There may, of course, still be some readers who remain skeptical with regard to the use of symbolism within the book of Revelation: How much symbolism is there? And how can we be assured that John's readers would have understood the book as having symbols?

To some extent, we have already begun to answer these questions. We have observed that the imagery of the book of Revelation is derived in large measure from the OT. We have also noticed that the imagery in Revelation is rooted in the finished work of Christ. We have seen that John used numbers in a symbolic manner in order to advance his narrative. And we have seen that the book of Revelation has an abundance of symbolism: lampstands, the Lion and the Lamb, the dragon, and more. Our look at symbolism in chapter 11 will endeavor to confirm that symbolism is a vital component to the book of Revelation.

Chapter 12 will examine the theme of holy war. Simply put, the book of Revelation is a war text. To understand the book of Revelation well, we will need to discern what holy war looked like and how it influenced John's writing. We will see that holy war is not what many might think it is. In Revelation's version of holy war, the victors are those who die—just as the Lion is the Lamb. Understanding the theme of holy war is important in that some of the imagery of the book of Revelation can only be understood when viewed from the perspective that John has used the theme of holy war.

Finally, in chapter 13 we will investigate the question of justice. The nature of the judgment scenes and the thought of God's vengeance naturally raises many questions for the modern reader. How do we reconcile the presence of wrath with the love of God, for instance? We will see that justice was a significant issue for John as well. Though a full theodicy is beyond the scope of an introductory book such as this, it will, nonetheless, be important to identify the basis for justice in the book of Revelation.

CHAPTER 10

Revelation and Dualism

John's use of dualism extends throughout the book of Revelation. David deSilva comments, "John's cosmos is a universe of stark alternatives. At every level of existence, there are two camps, and John has 'constructed his narrative world in such a way as to emphasize the mutual exclusivity of the two realms.'"[1]

John's use of dualism is of vital importance to understanding the book of Revelation. The failure to understand how John has used a dualistic framework leads to many of the most common interpretive mistakes. In this chapter we will look at how dualism works and its significance for our interpretation of the book of Revelation. We will save a number of examples of dualism for the For Further Study section at the end of the chapter. By doing so, the reader will be able to explore the significance of dualism for themselves.

DUALISM

Dualism is a common feature of apocalyptic writings. The primary manner in which dualism appears in the book of Revelation is the way in which John views the world in terms of two diametrically opposed kingdoms: the kingdom of the world and the kingdom of Christ. Of course, these two kingdoms are not equal. After all, the kingdom of God will overcome the world:

---

1. David deSilva, *Seeing Things John's Way: The Rhetoric of the Book of Revelation* (Louisville: Westminster John Knox, 2009), 112; citing Paul B. Duff, *Who Rides the Beast? Prophetic Rivalry and the Rhetoric of Crisis in the Churches of the Apocalypse* (New York: Oxford University Press, 2001), 76.

Then the seventh angel sounded; and there were loud voices in heaven, saying, "The kingdom of the world has become the kingdom of our Lord and of His Christ; and He will reign forever and ever." (11:15)

BEAST AND THE LAMB

The use of contrastive dualism between the beast and the Lamb is apparent in the description of the beast in Revelation 13. A first reading will likely alert most readers that the beast is the enemy of God's people. A more careful look at the beast, however, reveals that he is presented as a parody of Christ.

In popular thought the beast represents an anti-Christ character who is thought to be a political/world leader. These popular views suggest that the beast will come onto the world scene and demand worship. Understanding John's depiction of the beast in light of his consistent use of dualism leads to a markedly different conclusion.

That the beast is presented as a parody of Christ is evident primarily in the depiction of him in 13:3: "I saw one of his heads as if it had been slain, and his fatal wound was healed." That this contrast is intentional is shown by the fact that Jesus is described a few verses later as "the Lamb who has been slain" (13:8). Though some attempt to distinguish the beast from Christ on the basis that the beast only *seems* to have had a fatal wound,[2] the Greek text of Revelation does not afford us the opportunity to make such a distinction. The key here is that the description of the beast's being slain (or apparently slain) in 13:3 is identical to the description of Jesus (or the Lamb) in 5:6: "And I saw between the throne (with the four living creatures) and the elders a Lamb standing, as if slain."[3] It matters not whether

---

2. All of the major English translations render 13:3 with some form of qualifier that leaves the reader to conclude that perhaps the beast was not actually killed/slain—ESV: "seemed to have a mortal wound"; NET: "appeared to have been killed"; NIV: "seemed to have a fatal wound"; NKJV: "as if it had been mortally wounded"; NLT: "seemed wounded beyond recovery."

3. The translations are not attempting to sway the readers into thinking that the beast might not have been slain. The Greek text does appear to provide an initial impression that perhaps the beast was not slain and, as stated, the description in 13:3 is the same as that of Jesus in Revelation 5. Even if this is not noticed immediately, the rest of Revelation 13 makes it clear that the beast was, in fact, slain. See below.

the beast was actually slain. The key is that the beast is being described in the same manner as the Lamb.

We might be drawn to ask: Why was the Lamb described in language that leaves doubt as to whether or not He was actually killed? The answer is likely due to the nature of John's narrative (remember that Revelation is visionary literature more than it is a literal description of actual events). In Revelation 5, when John turns to look he saw a Lamb that appears to have been killed, but was clearly alive. Most readers of Revelation would have been well aware that the Lamb was indeed actually slain.

What about the beast? Was the beast actually killed? Before proceeding with this question, it is essential to remind ourselves of the nature of the book of Revelation and how this impacts our reading of the book. The question was the beast actually killed is a Western question. It is one that we are prone to ask. John and his first readers, however, were not Westerners. This question would not have arisen for them. Such a question makes the historical details of first importance, whereas for John and his readers it would have been the *literary* details that were most important.

When we examine this passage from its literary perspective the question of whether or not the beast was actually killed moves into the background. What comes to the forefront is the intended parody of the Lamb by the beast. Just as Jesus was dead and has come to life, so also the beast has died and come back to life. Of primary concern for John is that the beast is described in terms that have already been applied to Jesus—the beast is being depicted as a Christ-like figure.

The parallels between the beast and Jesus are heightened in the description that "his [the beast's] fatal wound was healed" (13:3). This is reiterated in 13:14, where it notes that the beast is the one who "had the wound of the sword and has come to life." This depiction is also of great significance because it further advances the notion that the beast is a Christ-like figure.

This should remind the reader of Jesus' warning that false prophets will appear in sheep's clothing (Matt. 7:15). In other words, false prophets look like us! They do not appear in secular society; they appear among the people of God. False prophets do not attempt to lead the world astray—after all the world is already deceived. Instead, false prophets attempt to deceive the people of God. Jesus says, "For false Christs and false prophets will arise and will show great signs and wonders, so as to mislead, if possible, even the elect" (Matt. 24:24).

FALSE PROPHET AND THE LAMB

That the beast parodies the Lamb is further accented by the description of the second beast (who is identified as "the false prophet"; cf. 16:13; 19:20; 20:10): "Then I saw another beast coming up out of the earth; and he had two horns like a lamb and he spoke as a dragon" (13:11). Both beasts have Christ-like features.

The application of this is straightforward. We know that the beast is evil and that we must be on our guard as he will attempt to infiltrate the people of God in order to lead us astray. If the beast were some political figure of worldwide importance who demanded worship, I do not suspect that many within the church would consider such a person a Christ figure.[4]

The danger is real for John. The church must be reminded: everyone whose name is not written in the Lamb's book of life will worship the beast (13:8). And anyone who "worships the beast and his image, and receives a mark on his forehead or upon his hand, he also will drink of the wine of the wrath of God" (14:9–10).

In the end, John notes the following:

> I saw the souls of those who had been beheaded because of their testimony of Jesus and because of the word of God, and those who had not worshiped the beast or his image, and had not received the mark on their forehead and on their hand; and they came to life and reigned with Christ for a thousand years. (20:4)

When reading Revelation 13 and the account of the beast, then, we must remember that though we, the readers of Revelation, know that the beast is empowered by the dragon and that he is the embodiment of evil, we must constantly be on our guard lest we allow the beast into our company.

---

4. Though history would warn us that political figures may be revered as divine—even by those who profess to be the church. Note that the description of the beast is meant as a warning to the people of God and that this is shown by the consistent reminder that those who have the mark of the beast will be condemned (cf. 14:9–10, 11; 16:2), while those who did not receive the mark will be rewarded (cf. 20:4–6; see also 15:2).

MARK OF THE BEAST AND THE SEAL OF GOD

To answer more fully the question of whether or not we have allowed the beast into our company, it is necessary to observe how John contrasts the "mark" of the beast and the "seal" of God.

That the mark of the beast is a parody of the seal of God is most evident from the narrative of 13:16–14:3. Though Revelation 13 and Revelation 14 are separated by a chapter break, it is clear that the 144,000 present on Mount Zion are set in contrast to those who have received the mark of the beast in 13:16–18.

This is evident from the fact that both the mark and the seal represent a "name" ("the name of the beast" 13:17; "His name and the name of His Father" 14:1). In addition, both the mark and the seal are said to be on the foreheads of those who receive them (7:3; 13:16; 22:4). In both cases it appears that they serve to provide certain benefits to those who have them (13:16–18; 7:13–17; 9:4). Note also the use of economic terms for each group. The mark of the beast enables one to participate in the economic system of the beast: "And he provides that no one will be able to buy or to sell, except the one who has the mark" (13:17). By contrast, those who have the seal of God are said to have been "purchased": "These have been purchased from among men as first fruits to God and to the Lamb" (14:4).

It is through understanding John's use of dualism, then, that we see the intended parody of the seal of God (7:2–8) by the mark of the beast (13:16–18).

CONCLUSION

As much as possible, I have deliberately avoided attempting to explain John's use of dualism in terms of a heaven-earth contrast. The danger in using such language in the modern world is that it reinforces a perspective that is prevalent among many Christians and is actually quite dangerous. This perspective tends to view the material world as evil and the heavenly, spiritual world as good. This approach is evident in popular writings on the book of Revelation and often results in an escapist approach to the world. It is my contention that this is precisely the opposite of John's view of things.

Thus, though it is appropriate to refer to the contrast in the book of Revelation in terms of the worldly kingdom of the beast versus the heavenly kingdom of Christ, I have refrained from doing so. The biblical distinction is that the kingdom of Christ will come down *from* heaven *to* the earth: "And I saw the holy city, new Jerusalem, coming down out of heaven from God" (21:2).

This is not escapism. The book of Revelation does not address a time when the Lord will return and deliver us from this world and take us to some heavenly kingdom. Instead, the book of Revelation addresses the role of God's people in the present: We are to be Christ's witnesses; we are to overcome. There, indeed, will be a day when Christ will come in justice and reward His people.

That day will be a day of resurrection!

For Further Study

1. It is easy for the readers of Revelation to conclude that the beast is evil. But when we consider John's description of the beast and how it has features that mimic Christ, is it possible that the description of the beast is so stark because some within the seven churches were in danger of being led astray by the beast? In what ways might the beast have infiltrated the church and appeared to many as Christ himself?

2. One of the more significant questions concerning the interpretation of the book of Revelation concerns the nature of the beasts in Revelation 13 and the mark of the beast (13:16–18). Compare and contrast the mark of the beast (13:16–18) and the seal of God (14:1–2). Note that chapter breaks would not have been present in the original. What might this mean for understanding the nature of the mark of the beast?

3. Examine references to "those who dwell on the earth" (3:10; 6:10; 8:13; 11:10 [twice]; 13:8; 13:12; 13:14 [twice]; 17:2; 17:8) and "those who dwell in heaven" (12:12; 13:6). Since the "hour of testing" (3:10) comes on "those who dwell on the earth," might it be that "those who dwell in heaven" is a contrastive way of referring to the people of God? What do we learn about each group?

4. Compare and contrast the harlot (17:1–18:24) and the bride (19:7–8; 21:9–22:5). We have already noted the "white garments" of the people of God. Observe the clothing of the harlot (17:4, 16). Note the use of "gold, precious stones, and pearls" (18:12, 16) as well as

"fine linen" (18:12, 16; 19:8, 14). What does this suggest about the harlot? (Hint: note the comments earlier in this chapter about false prophets and how they appear among the people of God).

5. Further contrasts between the harlot and the people of God can be seen in the use of "many waters." Examine the use of this phrase in Revelation (1:15; 14:2; 17:1; 19:6). Note that the "many waters" of 17:1 are interpreted for us in 17:15.

6. In addition to what we have already learned in this chapter, compare and contrast the beast from the sea (13:1–8) with the Lamb (5:5–6). What else does this mean for our understanding of the beast?

7. We have already observed the promise of "crowns" (2:10; 3:11; 4:4, 10). Note, however, that the rider on the white horse has "a crown" (6:2). Note, also, that the demonic hordes have "crowns" (9:7). Compare with the description of Christ in 19:11–16. In light of the discussion in this chapter, what might this mean for our understanding of the first rider and the demonic hordes?

8. Note that the one seated on the cloud in Revelation 14:14 also has a crown. How does this help/hinder our identification of this being? What does this tell us about the use of "crowns" throughout the book of Revelation?

9. One of the most significant contrasts in the book of Revelation occurs between the descriptions of the women in the book of Revelation. There are four women: Jezebel (2:20–23), the woman clothed with sun (12:1–17), the harlot (17:1–19:3), and the bride/holy city (21:1–22:5). In light of John's use of dualism, might we contend that there are only two women and not four? How does this help our understanding of the harlot?

Application

1. The book of Revelation portrays two competing kingdoms through the lens of Christ. Christ's kingdom, which is for all those who follow the Lamb, is the true victor. The reader of Revelation, however, must be warned: Even though Revelation portrays the beast as evil, we know that the beast deceives many. We must be reminded that the beast has many features that imitate Christ. Thus, for many,

the beast is alluring. When we add to this that the harlot is wealthy and prosperous, we may begin to realize how many, even those among the people of God, might be tempted to follow the beast. This might explain why John is so explicit in depicting the beast and the harlot as evil. The question for us then is this: What are some ways that the beast and the harlot tempt and deceive the people of God today?

CHAPTER 11

Revelation and Symbolism

The thought that Revelation uses symbolism might excite some. Others, however, may be skeptical. For them, acknowledging the presence of symbolism raises too many red flags: How do we determine what is symbolic and what is not? Who determines the meaning of the symbol? How do we know that that is the correct meaning?

In some respects the readers of this book have already been prepared for many of these questions. We have seen that discerning the meaning of the imagery in the book of Revelation is often quite simple. We have already noticed that the two keys for understanding the book of Revelation are that it is about Jesus and that its imagery is rooted in John's understanding of the fulfillment of the OT. Combining these two features provides the major controls for determining the meaning of the symbols in the book of Revelation. That is, John is (re)reading the OT story in light of its fulfillment in Jesus.

The book is about Jesus and the fulfillment of the OT narrative. For John, the OT narrative was weaving its way to fulfillment in Jesus. The promises of God to His people have been fulfilled in Him. With this conviction in mind, he explains to the seven churches what it all means for the church then and into the future.

REVELATION WAS "COMMUNICATED"

That the book of Revelation is a text steeped in symbolism is evident from the very first verse. The book of Revelation opens with the declaration "The Revelation of Jesus Christ, which God gave Him to show to His bond-servants, the things which must soon take place; and He sent and communicated it by His angel to His bond-servant John" (1:1). The word translated "communicated"[1] (*sēmainō*) in the NASB means "to make something clear; signify or show, especially by means of a sign."[2]

It is important to note that the noun form of this word (*sēmeion*) is used throughout the Gospels to indicate a sign or a symbol. Thus Judas' kiss of betrayal was a sign: "Now he who was betraying Him gave them a *sign*, saying, 'Whomever I kiss, He is the one; seize Him'" (Matt. 26:48, emphasis mine). In another example we see that the shepherds were told that "this will be a *sign* for you: you will find a baby wrapped in cloths and lying in a manger" (Luke 2:12, emphasis mine).

In the Gospel of John the noun *sēmeion* is also used to refer to Jesus' miracles (cf. John 2:11; 2:23; 4:54; 6:14). The Gospel of John, in fact, never refers to Jesus' miracles as miracles; they are always signs. The Gospel closes with the acknowledgment that "therefore many other *signs* Jesus also performed in the presence of the disciples, which are not written in this book" (John 20:30, emphasis mine). Earlier in the Gospel of John it states, "though He had performed so many *signs* before them, yet they were not believing in Him" (John 12:37, emphasis mine).[3]

The use of this term and its related noun form strongly supports the notion that when 1:1 says that God "communicated it by His angel to His bond-servant John," the means of that communication was through symbols.

THE USE OF SYMBOLS

That Revelation conveys its message to the churches through symbols is further substantiated by the fact that every time Revelation interprets itself it does so symbolically. For example, we are told this in Revelation 1:20:

---

1. NASB; cf. "made it known" (ESV, NIV); "made it clear" (NET); "signified it" (NKJV); "to present" (NLT).

2. See the context of Daniel 2:28–30, 45. The verbal form of this term occurs six times in the NT (John 12:33; 18:32; 21:19; Acts 11:28; 25:27; Rev. 1:1).

3. Throughout the four Gospels the noun form of this term is used exclusively in terms of "to show by means of a symbol." For example, in Matthew 12:38 the religious leaders tell Jesus that they "want to see a sign" to confirm His authority to do the things He was doing (cf. Matt. 16:1; Mark 8:11; Luke 11:16; John 2:18; 6:30); in Matthew 24:3 the disciples ask to know what "will be the sign of your coming?"(cf. Mark 13:4; Luke 21:7); in Matthew 24:24 Jesus explains that false prophets will perform many "signs" (cf. Mark 13:22).

As for the mystery of the seven stars which you saw in My right hand, and the seven golden lampstands: the seven stars are the angels of the seven churches, and the seven lampstands are the seven churches.

Later in Revelation 17 we are told:

Then one of the seven angels who had the seven bowls came and spoke with me, saying, "Come here, I will show you the judgment of the great harlot who sits on many waters.". . . And he said to me, "The waters which you saw where the harlot sits, are peoples and multitudes and nations and tongues." (17:1, 15)

These examples raise two basic possibilities. One option is that whenever the book of Revelation uses symbols it tells us. The idea behind this thought is that the book of Revelation is only using symbols when it explicitly says so. The common-sense element, of course, is that if the book of Revelation were not using symbols there would be no need to tell us. Nonetheless, this view is held by both those who tend to read the book of Revelation more literally and who advocate for the linear approach.

The problem here is that even proponents of this view are not consistent. After all, there are numerous examples in the book of Revelation in which imagery is used in a clearly symbolic manner even though John never tells us that it is symbolic. For example, John never explicitly tells us that the lion from the tribe of Judah (5:5) is not an actual lion; nor does he say that Satan is not actually a dragon (12:9).

The second basic possibility is that Revelation is modeling for us how to understand its language. When we are told that stars are angels and the lampstands are churches (1:20), the book of Revelation is showing us how to understand its message—namely, as a symbolical text. From this point forward we should assume that lampstands are churches and stars are angels.[4] This does not have to mean that stars are always angels.[5] But it does mean that we might start with the assumption that they are indeed angels.

---

4. It appears that stars indeed are most often angels in the book of Revelation. When a star is "coming down" they are good angels, but when they are "fallen" (e.g., 8:10; 9:1) they represent evil angels.

5. The instances in which stars are not to be understood as angels, but are indeed stars are usually quite obvious. For instance, when stars are referred to in a string that includes

That the book of Revelation uses symbols should not be much of a hindrance. We know without hesitation that Satan is not actually a seven-headed dragon (12:3–4). Neither should we assume that there is actually a woman clothed with the sun (12:1). Nor do we suspect that the harlot is actually an individual woman who sits atop a seven-headed beast (17:3). The people of God are not actually olive trees (11:4), any more than they are actually lampstands (11:4). Nor should we assume that the people of God are actually spewing fire out of their mouths (11:5). And so on. The meaning of the symbols is often quite evident.[6]

What I hope to have demonstrated in this book is the fact that much of the symbolism of the book of Revelation can be well understood. Most importantly, the message of the book of Revelation can be well understood. Therefore, the book of Revelation can be read and understood and used in the church even if we cannot determine with any consensus who the beast is. What we can agree upon is that the beast appears to be an agent of Satan who wages war against God's people: "It was also given to him to make war with the saints and to overcome them" (13:7).

CONCLUSION

I have saved the discussion of symbolism in the book of Revelation until this point of our study for an important reason: saving it until this point has allowed us to see that the book is clearly symbolic. That is, it is not so necessary now to argue that such is the case, for we have already seen that it is so.

Viewing Revelation in light of its rich symbolism allows the book of Revelation to have its greatest impact: beasts are evil; harlots sitting on beasts are evil. Those who wish to decode the book of Revelation spend too much time attempting to discern who or what is represented by the harlot who sits astride the beast. The problem with this approach is that the book of Revelation is stripped of one of its greatest features—its ability to affect our emotions.

---

the sun and the moon (e.g., 6:12–13; 8:12; 12:1) it is quite apparent that stars mean stars. The only occurrence of stars that is really in question is in 12:4, but even there it likely refers to angels (fallen ones at that).

6. This is not to deny that there are several crucial instances in which the meaning of the symbols is not only unclear, but even disputed by many—especially when it comes to the nature of the beast (13:1–8)

Instead of spending an exorbitant amount of time attempting to decode the seven heads and ten horns of the beast, it seems more fitting that the people of God use this time to be prepared: "Stay awake!" as John tells us (16:15).

John has woven a literary masterpiece, and his use of symbolism clothes it as a work of art.

For Further Study

1. The symbolism of the book of Revelation is perhaps the most difficult element of the book. In light of what we have learned throughout our study, including the present chapter about the nature of symbolism in the book of Revelation, why is it important to understand the symbolism as symbolism instead of imposing literalistic assumptions on the text?

2. Observe that the first indication of white garments is in 3:4 where the faithful in Sardis are encouraged by the fact that "they will walk with Me in white." What is the significance of this promise?

3. Observe that Christ is said to have a "robe" (1:13), though it is not said to be white. What might be the significance of this? Hint: note that the garments of the people of God have been made white "in the blood of the Lamb" (7:14).

4. The term "wilderness" occurs three times in the book of Revelation. Its meaning in the first two occurrences (12:6, 14) appears to be straightforward, corresponding to the OT wilderness where the Israelites were both nourished and tested. The third occurrence, however, seems to be somewhat at odds with this. Revelation 17:3 says that John is taken to the wilderness where he sees a harlot. Examine the use of wilderness in these three passages and its verbal cognate ("lay waste/desolate") in 17:16; 18:17, 19. What do you think is the significance of the fact that John is taken to the wilderness to see the harlot?

5. Compare and contrast the harlot Babylon (17–18) and the new Jerusalem (21–22). Note that both are cities and both are presented as women. Note the final destiny of each. What might this mean for our understanding of each? What is the temptation that leads people to follow the harlot? What sort of people enter the new Jerusalem?

6. Is it possible that some of the symbols may have more than one referent? That is, could it be that the beast and the harlot may have represented something real and substantive to John's readers/hearers and yet represent something else real and substantive to us today?

Application

1. Though it might be helpful to know who the beast is, the book of Revelation simply alerts us that the people of God have some beast-like thing that makes war with them. What do you think is the significance of this for the life of God's people today?

CHAPTER 12

Revelation and Holy War

Spoiler Alert! Christ wins. Sorry if I took all the drama and anxiety away. But in all reality, I am not sure I spoiled anything—the theme of holy war underlies the book of Revelation. This does not mean that Revelation describes some final, cataclysmic battle as some suppose. The theme of holy war merely serves as the clothing with which the book is dressed. After all, the means by which Christ, who is Himself the holy warrior, wins are not through actual warfare, but sacrificial surrender. Love is Christ's weapon of choice.

By portraying matters from the perspective of conflict, John is able to draw a clear line between the people of God and those who dwell on the earth. For John, one cannot become followers of both the beast and the Lamb. They are on two opposing sides of a cosmic battle.

WAR IN THE BOOK OF REVELATION

Though many believe that history will close with an apocalyptic, final battle, Armageddon, many readers will be surprised to learn that the book of Revelation does not describe any such battle. Some of you may have put this book down for a minute or more to go look through the book of Revelation, sure that you could find a multitude of references to such a war. However, you will find no such descriptions! The book of Revelation appears to set the stage for such battles—armies even assemble to wage war against Christ. But the book of Revelation never describes an actual battle. It does, however, relate the *outcome* of such a battle: Christ wins!

The closest the book of Revelation comes to describing an actual battle is in Revelation 17:14:

These [the beast and the kings of the earth] will wage war against
the Lamb, and the Lamb will overcome them, because He is Lord
of lords and King of kings, and those who are with Him are the
called and chosen and faithful.

Note that there is no description of a battle here. The beast and the
kings of the earth assemble to wage war against Christ and they are destroyed. No details. No depiction of a battle or any long, drawn-out war.
Consider Revelation 20:

And when the thousand years are completed, Satan will be released from his prison, and will come out to deceive the nations
which are in the four corners of the earth, Gog and Magog, to
gather them together for the war; the number of them is like the
sand of the seashore. And they came up on the broad plain of the
earth and surrounded the camp of the saints and the beloved city.
(20:7–9a)

Here, again, the reader is set for an intense description of this final
battle. The devil has gathered his army and surrounded the people of God.
The stage is set. Then John declares, "and fire came down from heaven and
devoured them" (20:9b).

How anti-climactic can you get? What a letdown—at least for the readers
who were expecting some detailed description of the world's greatest battle.
All they get is "fire came down from heaven and devoured them." Imagine
if the movie *Gladiator* ended without the final fight scene in the Coliseum.
The movie has brought us to this climatic moment. The crowds are going
crazy. The dignitaries take their seats. The music builds and the suspense
draws us in. The fighters have entered the arena and are prepared for the
duel of the ages. Then "fire comes down from heaven," destroys everyone,
and the credits role. It probably would not be a box office sensation. It sure
makes for a poor ending to a movie. But it sounds great for God's people!

The book of Revelation is not concerned with such details. The point is
not to describe some final, literal battle that takes place at the end of time.
After all, I do not suppose that God revels in the destruction of His enemies. As the prophet Ezekiel affirms, "'For I have no pleasure in the death
of anyone who dies,' declares the Lord GOD. 'Therefore, repent and live'"

(Ezek. 18:32). And if God does not revel in the details of a bloody war, then neither should we.

There is another reason why I suppose the book of Revelation does not depict the details of a final war, namely, that the book of Revelation is more concerned with the present. John wants his readers to know and understand something in order that they might overcome and fulfill the mission for which they have been called.

Knowledge that, in the end, Satan and all those who side with him will be destroyed should be enough to motivate the people of God to act in the present. There is no need for any gruesome details of their destruction. It is sufficient that

> the devil who deceived them was thrown into the lake of fire and brimstone, where the beast and the false prophet are also; and they will be tormented day and night forever and ever. . . . Then death and Hades were thrown into the lake of fire. This is the second death, the lake of fire. And if anyone's name was not found written in the book of life, he was thrown into the lake of fire. (20:10, 14–15)

This reality should even create a measure of grief for John's readers. We might want to stop every time we come to a passage such as this and pray for those whom we know and love, those whom we do not know, and for anyone whom we fear might suffer the fate describe here.

There is one more reason why I suppose the book of Revelation does not give any details of an apocalyptic, end-times war that ends it all: there will not be any such war. If we stop and think about it, the battle is not fair. One side has way too much going for it. It is kind of like picking kids for a baseball team: one team was comprised of all the kindergartners while the other squad was picking players from the professional ranks. In the war of Revelation, the side that has Christ is going to win—it is not even going to be a contest! That is why the book of Revelation does not describe any long, drawn-out final battle.

HOLY WAR IN THE BOOK OF REVELATION

The theme of holy war pervades the book of Revelation. In fact, Revelation can well be described as a war text. This might seem out of place to some—war texts belong in the OT, or not in Scripture at all. Nonetheless, key aspects of holy war help illuminate the book of Revelation.

Jesus as a Holy Warrior

The most obvious element of holy war in the book of Revelation is the portrayal of Christ as a holy warrior in Revelation 19:11–16. This is the significance of Christ on a white horse. Such horses were what kings and generals rode into battle. Jesus is depicted here in terms of a Roman general who is coming to wage war, to establish His rule, and to capture and punish His enemies, the dragon and the two beasts.

The People of God as Holy Warriors

The book of Revelation also portrays the people of God as holy warriors. This is, among other things, the significance of the numbering of the 144,000. The only other occasion in all of Scripture in which God approves the counting of the people of God is in the book of Numbers (cf. Num. 1:3, 18, 20; 26:2, 4).[1] Since the census in Numbers is directly tied to the assembling of an army, it is reasonable to suppose the purpose for numbering the 144,000 in Revelation 7 is also to determine the military strength of the people of God.[2]

That the people of God are described as a holy army is also supported by the description of them as such at the second coming of Christ. John observes, "And the armies which are in heaven, clothed in fine linen, white and clean, were following Him on white horses" (19:14).

In addition, we see that the 144,000 are described as "the ones who have not been defiled with women, for they have kept themselves chaste" (14:4a). That they "have not been defiled with women" corresponds with the military code in the OT law in which men were not permitted to have sexual relations during warfare.[3] The 144,000, then, are depicted as the people of God who are faithful during military warfare.

---

1. Note that there were other censuses taken in the OT (1 Chron. 21:5; 27:23; 2 Sam. 24:9). These too were to count the men of military age. The census in Numbers is the only occasion, however, in which God approved.

2. Bauckham says that "a census is always a counting up of the *military* strength of the nation" (emphasis original). *Climax of Prophecy* (Edinburgh: T&T Clark, 2000), 217.

3. Cf. Deuteronomy 23:9–14. This is why Uriah refused to have sex with his wife Bathsheba after David called him home. Since David had impregnated his wife, he was

Warfare with Grace

Of course, one cannot read the book of Revelation as simply an ancient war text. The message of Revelation is not primarily about war, but about grace. The very nations who suffer at the hand of the One who rides the white horse are themselves the focus of God's grace.

Thus the delay in Christ's return appears to be based on the desire for God to give grace that the nations might repent. The desire to give grace likely explains why it takes so long for vengeance to arrive in the narrative of Revelation. The souls who had been slain cry out in chapter 6 for vengeance (6:10), yet they are told to wait a while longer (6:11).

The desire to give grace may also account for the fact that the destruction of the seven trumpets is only partial. After the description of the first six trumpets, we learn that the nations still did not repent (9:20–21). Was the destruction partial because God was sparing the rest in order that they might repent?

It is only when we reach the climactic series of seven bowls (15:1–16:21) that there appears to be no more time for repentance:

> Then one of the four living creatures gave to the seven angels seven golden bowls full of the wrath of God, who lives forever and ever. And the temple was filled with smoke from the glory of God and from His power; and no one was able to enter the temple until the seven plagues of the seven angels were finished. (15:7–8)

Since we know that the prayers have been placed at the altar (cf. 8:3–4), it appears that the inability for anyone to enter the temple suggests that with the seven bowls there is no more opportunity to repent.

CONCLUSION

The question we must ask about the holy war is what does John want his readers to know? It appears that John first wants his readers—and, of course, those in the generations to follow—to know that we are at war with the devil—or, perhaps, it might be better stated that the devil

---

hoping that Uriah would sleep with her and then later think the child was his own. David, however, did not account for Uriah's righteous adherence to the law, which denied Israelites the right to have sex during war.

is at war with us. This present war necessitates God's people to be prepared. This is vital to reading, understanding, and applying the book of Revelation. I pray that every reader of this book learns well the biblical principle, which is well narrated in the book of Revelation, that the people of God are the focus of the dragon and the beast's war against God.

Second, John wants his readers to know that they must stand firm because they are on the winning side. The details describing the victory of a final battle that is won by God's people are not necessary. What is necessary is that Christ wins. And "those who are with Him are the called and chosen and faithful" (17:14).

As for the nature of this war, we might first note that it is not what one expects. Surely, God will bring, and in fact is already bringing, justice. The real goal, however, is that someday there will be

> a great multitude which no one could count, from every nation and all tribes and peoples and tongues, standing before the throne and before the Lamb, clothed in white robes, and palm branches were in their hands; and they cry out with a loud voice, saying, "Salvation to our God who sits on the throne, and to the Lamb." (7:9–10)

And we hope and pray that our loved ones and everyone, even our enemies, are part of this group.

This is not to say that the theme of holy war is not present in the book of Revelation, but only that there is no final climatic battle.[4] The opponents of Christ will wage war against the people of God. Once Christ appears, however, the battle is over. Those who are expecting some literal war on a battlefield in the Middle East will indeed be disappointed. Those who want God to lay waste to His enemies in the present will be disappointed. For when God wages war it is with the goal of redemption. He fights not simply to enact vengeance, but to bring repentance.

---

4. For those wondering how the battle of Armageddon fits into this, see Appendix 3.

For Further Study

1. That Christ is portrayed as a holy warrior is evident from the descriptions of Jesus in 19:11–16. Examine this passage and describe how Christ fits the description of a holy warrior.

2. In some of the OT holy war traditions God wins alone (cf. Exod. 14:13–14; 2 Kings 19:32–35; Isa. 37:33–36) and in others He wins with his heavenly army (cf. Zech. 14:5).[5] Which portrayal does the book of Revelation take?

3. In light of the fact that those "who follow the Lamb" (14:4) are associated with the holy army, and in view of Revelation's understanding of Jesus as victorious through death (5:5–6), what does this mean for the life of the Christian today?[6]

4. The expression "new song" (5:9; 14:3) refers to a song of praise to God after a military victory (note that 15:3 refers to the song of Moses in Exod. 15:1–18, which itself was a song of praise to God after the victory at the Red Sea). Note that the song of Revelation 5:9–10 connects Christ's victory with His death. In light of this, read Revelation 15–16. What does this mean for our understanding of the account of the seven bowls—that is, how do they fit into the narrative of the book of Revelation?

5. The theme of holy war in the NT is not limited to the book of Revelation. What are some other passages in the NT that make sense in light of the theme of holy war?

6. What might it mean that the beast will overcome the two witnesses (11:7)?[7]

---

5. See Bauckham, *Climax of Prophecy*, 210–11.

6. Note that this may be one of the most important questions in our study of Revelation.

7. Note that the two witnesses likely represent the entirety of the people of God. They are certainly more than two people. After all, they are portrayed as "two lampstands" (11:4). And we know that lampstands represent churches and not distinct individuals.

Application

1. In light of the fact that Revelation consistently exhorts the people of God to overcome and that the book may be described as a war text, what does this mean for Christian living?

2. What are some ways that the people of God are at war with the devil today? What are some of the most effective ways to combat the devil?

3. What are some wars that the church is fighting today in which we might be better served by not fighting?

CHAPTER 13

Revelation and Justice

One of the issues that any study of Revelation needs to address, especially in the twenty-first century, is that of God's justice. Some readers are already thrown off by the thought that the book of Revelation is about God's wrath upon the world. What is errant in this understanding of the book of Revelation, however, is that, though the wrath of God on the world is present in the book of Revelation, it is not by any means the focus.[1] The focus, rather, is upon God's people. John writes to the churches to encourage, exhort, and warn them: the churches are encouraged with the reminder that God has fulfilled His promises in Christ. They are exhorted to carry out God's mission to the world and to overcome the dangers and temptations that confront them. And they are warned of the perils that await those who do not overcome.

As we read the narrative of the book of Revelation we learn that this mission to which God has called His people will have tremendous opposition. We learn from the seven letters of Revelation 2–3 that opposition will be from within as false teachers attempt to infiltrate the people of God in an effort to lead them astray. Opposition will also come from without as Satan empowers the kings of the earth to oppose God's people. Throughout all this the people of God are to maintain their witness and fulfill their mission in the face temptation and suffering, knowing that God will redeem and reward them. They too will be resurrected (11:11–12).

---

1. One motivation for this misunderstanding is the common idea that Revelation is primarily about "the end of the world." For further discussion of this point—in what sense Revelation is and in what sense it is not about the end of the world—see Appendix 4.

The focus of Revelation, then, is to encourage and exhort God's people: Hang in there and overcome, because the One who is "the firstborn of the dead" (1:5), and has "the keys of death and Hades" (1:18), and who Himself "was dead" and is "alive forevermore" (1:18) will also resurrect you!

The goal in Revelation is not the destruction of the enemies of God's people. The goal, rather, is the redemption of the nations. That someday "the nations will walk by its light, and the kings of the earth will bring their glory into it" (21:24).

At the same time, however, the people of God are encouraged to remain faithful, knowing that their enemies will be defeated and judged. The final destiny of those who refuse to repent is an important element in Revelation's narrative—there is much rejoicing in heaven at the destruction of Babylon (18:20; 19:1–6). In such instances of portrayed judgment, the focus is not so much on those who are judged as it is on the people of God being vindicated and the destruction of the evil institutions that oppress them.

For John, the knowledge that God will judge the enemies of God's people is intended to encourage his readers to persevere a little longer. For those who are waning in their faithfulness to God and in danger of compromising their faith, John writes to warn them not to side with the dragon, the beast, the false prophet, or the nations, because their end is the lake of fire.

JUSTICE IN THE BOOK OF REVELATION

That the nations are punished by God is certainly an important component of the narrative in Revelation. The book of Revelation, however, does not describe God as some Almighty Being waiting to dispense justice upon those who oppose Him. Instead, justice, as I noted in our discussion of holy war, is always in accordance with grace.

There are two important considerations when it comes to the issue of justice in the book of Revelation—and even in the whole of Scripture. First, God prefers that the nations repent and receive grace. Second, those who receive justice are receiving what they have dispensed—that is, God treats them precisely as they have treated His people. Ultimately, the fate of humankind rests upon each person's attitude and actions toward God.

And one's attitude and actions toward God are manifested in the way one treats His people.[2]

LEX TALIONIS

The principle of *lex talionis* undergirds the issue of justice in the book of Revelation. This principle, which is often cited as "an eye for an eye and a tooth for a tooth," forms the basis of the OT law. God is not haphazardly dispensing justice. He is not an evil ogre who wants all men to fear Him or suffer. Instead, He is simply giving back to those who do not wish to repent what they have themselves done to God's people.

This principle, which is found throughout the Scriptures, is readily apparent in Jesus' parable of the sheep and the goats (cf. Matt. 25:31–46). At the conclusion of the parable, Jesus states, "Truly I say to you, to the extent that you did it to one of these brothers of Mine, even the least of them, you did it to Me" (Matt. 25:40).

"Poured Out"

In the book of Revelation, the principle that God's treatment of the nations directly parallels how the nations have treated God's people is most explicit in the account of the seven bowls (Revelation 16). The narrative of

---

2. This is an important distinction for many evangelicals. The principle is simple: how one treats God's people is how one treats God. As we will see, this is the basis for the judgment of the nations in the book of Revelation. It is apparent in the parable of the sheep and the goats in Matthew 25. In the OT the same principle is found in the promise to Abraham in Genesis 12:1–3: those who bless Abraham and his offspring will be blessed and those who curse them will be cursed. The blessing or cursing that comes from how one treats Abraham's offspring in the OT era is not due to their racial identity. Instead, it is due to the fact that the offspring of Abraham are His chosen people. One's conduct towards them was thus equated with one's conduct towards God—the One who chose them. As we move into the NT we see that Jesus redefines family not according to racial lines but according to one's allegiance to Jesus. He says that his mother and sister and brother are "whoever does the will of God" (Mark 3:35; cf. Matt. 12:50). That is, the OT principle concerning how one treats God's people (Abraham and his offspring) is continued in the NT. The only distinction is that in the NT God's people are defined not by race but by faith, which one could argue was actually the case in the OT era as well. After all, not all Abraham's descendants were part of the chosen race, and others who were not physical descendants of Abraham (Uriah the Hittite, Rahab, Ruth) were included in the family of God. For more on this topic and the implications for contemporary struggles, see my *These Brothers of Mine* (Eugene, OR: Wipf & Stock, 2011), and Gary Burge, *Whose Land? Whose Promise?* (Cleveland: Pilgrim Press, 2003).

the seven bowls begins with a clear command to each of the seven angels to "pour out" their bowls (16:1),[3] which they subsequently do (16:2, 3, 4, 8, 10, 12, 17). After the third bowl is emptied an angel declares:

> Righteous are You, who are and who were, O Holy One, because You judged these things; for they *poured out* the blood of saints and prophets, and You have given them blood to drink. They deserve it. (16:5–6, emphasis mine)

What is essential for us to note is that the exact same verb (Greek *ekcheō*) is used in Revelation 16:6 as is used in Revelation 16:2, 3, 4, 8, 10, 12, and 17. What the seven bowls confirm, then, is that the angels "pour out" their bowls on the nations because the nations have "poured out" the blood of God's people.[4]

Revelation 16 is clear: the wrath of God upon the nations directly corresponds to the way the nations have treated His people.

The Trampling of God's People

That the wrath of God upon the nations corresponds directly to the treatment of God's people is also seen in the account of the two witnesses (11:1–13). At the end of chapter 10 John is told that he must prophesy concerning the nations (10:11). Then, in the opening of Revelation 11 he is given a measuring rod. In Scripture, a measuring rod is given to a prophet to measure something often as a symbol of divine protection for what is

---

3. All of the major English translations render the verb "poured out" (Greek *ekcheō*) here and throughout Revelation 16.

4. Despite the fact that all of the major English translation have rendered the verb "poured out" when it refers to the seven angels pouring out their bowls, the ESV, NIV, NKJV, and NLT have chosen to translate this verb as "they have shed the blood. . ." in Revelation 16:6. The problem is that, although the translation "they have shed the blood . . ." (ESV, NIV, NKJV, and NLT) is a very good rendering of the Greek, it fails to maintain a consistency in translation that is vital for a complete understanding of the text. The ESV, NIV, NKJV, and NLT's translation of 16:6 make it clear that the nations have killed ("shed the blood of") God's people. But we could easily have discerned that this is what the text meant by the translation "they poured out the blood of" as NASB and NET have rendered it. The advantage of the NASB and NET translation here is that those without the ability to read the Greek text are better able to see what John is doing. John wants his readers to know that God's authorization of the angels to "pour out" the bowls is directly the result of the fact that the nations have "poured out" the blood of God's people.

measured.[5] John is told that he must "rise and measure the temple, the altar, and the worshipers" (11:1, my translation),[6] thus signifying that the temple, the altar, and the worshipers are under God's protection.[7]

As the narrative of Revelation 11 continues we see that John is then strikingly told not to measure the outer court because "it has been given to the nations, and they will tread underfoot the holy city for forty-two months" (11:2). What might this mean? Well, without laboring too deeply into a detailed examination of this passage,[8] the basic meaning here is that though the people of God are protected—which is signified by the fact that the "worshipers" are measured—they, or perhaps some of them, will still suffer persecution at the hands of the nations.

The narrative of Revelation 11 then depicts the ministry of the two witnesses (11:3–14). When these two witnesses finish their prophetic ministry they are killed by the beast (11:7). Their deaths, however, result in their

---

5. For a discussion of measuring in prophetic and apocalyptic literature, see my *Revelation and the Two Witnesses* (Eugene, OR: Wipf & Stock, 2011), 4–6.

6. Note that the NIV (prior to its recent revision) and the NLT both translated 11:1 somewhat strangely. Almost all English translations render the verse very closely to the Greek: "rise and measure the temple of God, and the altar, and those who worship in it" (my translation, which matches very closely with the ESV, NASB, NET, and the NKJV). The old NIV and the NLT add a verb at the end of the verse to their translation that is not in the Greek text, leaving us with: "and count the worshipers there" (old NIV). The reason why they have done this is that the Greek leaves one puzzled as to what John could possibly mean. The command to measure the temple and the altar is understandable. For one can easily see how John could use a measuring rod to measure the temple and the altar. The last clause, however, is strange. It appears that John is commanded to also measure "the worshipers." But how does one measure people (i.e., the worshipers)? This question has caused the old NIV and the NLT to add the verb "count" before "the worshipers." That is, the worshipers are not measured, they are counted. But the text does not say they are counted. The Greek here is quite clear: John is told to "rise" (or "get up") and "measure" three items: the first direct object is "the temple of God," which is followed by an "and"; the second item, "the altar," which is also followed by an "and"; and then the third item, "those who worship in it." If we understand the act of measuring in terms of a prophetic act that indicates the divine protection of what is measured, as it is used in the prophetic literature, then we should have no problem wondering why John is told to measure the worshipers: they are measured because they too are under God's sovereign protection. Trying to impose a level of wooden literalism on an apocalyptic writing forced the translators to unnecessarily add a verb that is not present.

7. We should note that the temple of God is used throughout the NT to represent either the body of Christ Himself or the people of God (see Matt. 26:61; 1 Cor. 3:16, 17; 1 Cor. 6:19; 2 Cor. 6:16).

8. For a detailed look at Revelation 11, see my *Revelation and the Two Witnesses*.

resurrection (11:12). Thus, in accordance with the message of the book of Revelation, we learn that the people of God, despite being killed, are the ones who rise.

The narrative of Revelation 11 continues into Revelation 12, 13, and 14. In Revelation 12 and 13 we learn that Satan is the ultimate source of the war against God's people. It is Satan (the dragon) who authorizes the beast to wage war against them (13:7). In Revelation 14, we learn that, despite the great war against God's people, it is they who are ultimately with Christ (14:1).

Nations Are Trampled

The episode concludes in Revelation 14 with a depiction of two harvests. Each harvest begins when an angel is commanded to swing a sharp sickle and reap (14:15, 18).[9] The first angel swings his sickle and reaps, suggesting some sort of grain harvest. The second swings and gathers grapes. The gathered grapes are then "thrown into the great wine press of the wrath of God" (14:19). As we saw in chapter 4, these are two harvests, not one. In Scripture grain harvests tend to be depictions of the harvesting of the people of God (Matt. 13:24–30, 36-43), whereas grape harvests, and the accompanying trampling of the grapes, are common depictions of the judgment of God upon the nations (cf. Joel 3:13; Jer. 25:30).[10]

How does all this relate to the principle of *lex talionis?* Quite simply, the nations have "tread under foot" the people of God (11:2) and as a consequence the grapes are "trodden" (14:20). A quick look at the Greek lying behind both Revelation 11:2 and 14:20 confirms that both passages use the same verb (*pateō*). This means that the punishment of the nations stems from the manner in which they have treated God's people. In the narrative of Revelation 11–14 John reminds his readers that, though the nations presently tread upon God's people, in the end it is God who will tread upon the nations.

God's Judgment and Justice

This raises an important question, Is God just? The wrath of God against the dragon, the beast, and the false prophet may seem warranted. But what

---

9. Whether the first "angel" in Revelation 14:14–16 is an angel or Christ is debated.
10. See chapter 4 for more discussion.

about the nations? This question, which in many ways has become even more central to a millennial generation that prides itself on its concern for justice, has always been relevant. Revelation's effort to address the justice of God confirms that this question was likely present in the minds of John's readers as well.

In order to adequately understand the book of Revelation's answer to this question it is essential to note two fundamental elements of Revelation's narrative. First, the nations are provided with ample opportunities to repent. This, in fact, is one of the primary emphases in Revelation. God sends His people to the nations in order that the nations might know and repent. And in the end, many do repent. Thus, the new Jerusalem is where

> The nations will walk by its light, and the kings of the earth will bring their glory into it. In the daytime (for there will be no night there) its gates will never be closed; and they will bring the glory and the honor of the nations into it. (21:24–26)

Second, those who face God's wrath do so explicitly because they refused to repent. This also is stressed throughout the book of Revelation:

> The rest of humankind, who were not killed by these plagues, did not repent of the works of their hands, so as not to worship demons, and the idols of gold and of silver and of brass and of stone and of wood, which can neither see nor hear nor walk; and they did not repent of their murders nor of their sorceries nor of their immorality nor of their thefts. (9:20–21)

> Men were scorched with fierce heat; and they blasphemed the name of God who has the power over these plagues, and they did not repent so as to give Him glory. (16:9)

> Then the fifth angel poured out his bowl on the throne of the beast, and his kingdom became darkened; and they gnawed their tongues because of pain, and they blasphemed the God of heaven because of their pains and their sores; and they did not repent of their deeds. (16:10–11)

CONCLUSION

The wrath of God is indeed present in the book of Revelation. It is not, however, the emphasis. Revelation's warning about the wrath of God is not intended to compel non-Christians to belief. After all, non-Christians are not likely to read the book. Instead, it was designed as a source of comfort and as a warning to the people of God: (1) persevere—for God will soon vindicate the people of God, and (2) persevere—for judgment will come upon all those who refuse to repent.

For Further Study

1. The book of Revelation consistently portrays God as righteous in His judgments.[11] See 15:3, 4; 16:5, 7; and 19:2. Why do suppose this was important to John? After reading the book of Revelation, consider whether God just in His judgments.

2. In our chapter on the narrative of Revelation (chap. 9) we noticed that there was a delay in the response to the prayers of the saints. What caused that delay and how does this affect our understanding of justice in the book of Revelation?

3. The description of the new Jerusalem says that "the nations will walk by its light" (21:24). What are some of the possible explanations for this, and what might this mean for our understanding of judgment in the book of Revelation?

4. Amos 4:1–13 describes God's acts of judgment upon Israel and that they were intended to bring Israel to repentance. Note that neither the judgments in Amos nor those in Revelation appear to bring the nations to repentance (9:20–21). What then is the key to bring the nations to repentance?

5. The result of the second seal is that "men should slay one another" (6:4). Look at the other instances of the verb "slay" (*sphazō*) in the book of Revelation (5:6, 9, 12; 6:4, 9; 13:3, 8; 18:24) and discern how this word is used (i.e., who are those who are slain?). What is the only exception among these verses? What might account for

---

11. The word "righteous" is sometimes rendered "just" by some translations. The ESV, NET, NIV, and NLT, for instance, use "just" in 16:5 where others translate the same word "righteous."

this exception (hint: see chap. 10 of this study)? What does this mean for our understanding of the seven seals?

Application

1. As mentioned in this chapter, the book of Revelation was not written to unbelievers. Thus the judgments in the book cannot have been meant as a warning to the those who follow the beast. What, then, is the significance for believers and unbelievers of the judgment of God in the book of Revelation?

Conclusion to Part 4

We have seen that in order to fully comprehend the book of Revelation we must recognize its dualistic framework. For John, there is good and evil. There is the King of kings with "many diadems" (19:12), and there is the beast who has "ten diadems" (13:1). This false claimant demands allegiance. The question for John's readers, and for us today, is whether we will "follow the Lamb" or "worship the beast."

In addition, we have learned throughout our study that the book of Revelation is immersed with symbolic language. The symbolism, as we learned in chapter 4, derives primarily from the OT.

We have also seen that the book of Revelation is cast in the mold of holy war. This does not mean that the book of Revelation depicts a physical war as many might suspect. Instead, the battle, though quite real, is waged by the devil against Christ and the people of God. This war will be won by Christ.

Finally, we addressed the ever-present issue of God's justice. We have seen that God appears to delay His justice in order that the nations might repent. At the same time, we have seen that the justice of God on the nations is His response to the nations' treatment of the people of God.

Epilogue

To read, understand, and apply the book of Revelation well we must understand that the book is about Jesus. John is reading the OT through the lens of Jesus: He has fulfilled the Scriptures. He has overcome. He was dead and now is alive. He has the keys of death and Hades. He is the Lion of the tribe of Judah. He is the returning king.

And He has called us to be kings. We must overcome! We are lampstands that must shine to the nations and hold fast the testimony of Jesus and the word of God. And this may well cost us our lives.

Revelation reminds us that we have an adversary. This adversary does not play fair. He follows no rules. What he apparently fails to comprehend is that the shed blood of the people of God is their means of victory. Just as the Lion has overcome by being the slain Lamb, so also the people of God will hear "come up here" (11:12).

In the end, we are reminded that those who follow the Lamb are

the ones who come out of the great tribulation, and they have washed their robes and made them white in the blood of the Lamb. For this reason, they are before the throne of God; and they serve Him day and night in His temple; and He who sits on the throne will spread His tabernacle over them. They will hunger no longer, nor thirst anymore; nor will the sun beat down on them, nor any heat; for the Lamb in the center of the throne will be their shepherd, and will guide them to springs of the water of life; and God will wipe every tear from their eyes. (7:14–17)

And they are encouraged that soon

the tabernacle of God is among men, and He will dwell among them, and they shall be His people, and God Himself will be among them, and He will wipe away every tear from their eyes; and there will no longer be any death; there will no longer be any mourning, or crying, or pain; the first things have passed away. . . . Then he showed me a river of the water of life, clear as crystal, coming from the throne of God and of the Lamb, in the middle of its street. On either side of the river was the tree of life, bearing twelve kinds of fruit, yielding its fruit every month; and the leaves of the tree were for the healing of the nations. There will no longer be any curse; and the throne of God and of the Lamb will be in it, and His bond-servants will serve Him; they will see His face, and His name will be on their foreheads. And there will no longer be any night; and they will not have need of the light of a lamp nor the light of the sun, because the Lord God will illumine them; and they will reign forever and ever. (21:3–4; 22:1–5)

There is no better way to close our study than by affirming with John himself: "He who testifies to these things says, 'Yes, I am coming quickly.' Amen. Come, Lord Jesus. The grace of the Lord Jesus be with all. Amen" (22:20–21).

Symbolism and the Popular Understanding of Revelation

Many evangelicals today have been influenced by the countless popular works written on the book of Revelation. These writings assume that the book of Revelation presents us with a detailed description of the future. Such writings often suggest that John saw visions of the future, which some contend included images of nuclear war and a great cataclysmic battle. These popular writers then suppose that John did his best to relay these visions to his first-century readers in the language he had available to him. Some of these writers, furthermore, claim that these visions can only be understood by the generation in which the fulfillment comes—that is, not until the events in Revelation begin to occur will its meaning be fully understood. Of course, for most of these popular writers, we just so happen to be the lucky generation.[1]

According to these end-times "experts," for instance, the sky rolling up like a scroll (6:14) is John's effort to describe a mushroom cloud after

---

1. Such authors regularly assume that the "future" that John was viewing is their "present." This is a common mistake made throughout the centuries by so-called prophecy experts. It need not be noted that every prophetic pundit in the history of the church who has predicted the timing of the second coming of Christ has been wrong (of course, those who are presently predicting the return of Christ have not yet been proven wrong, but if we simply look at history it is quite reasonable to surmise that they too will be proven wrong). This should cause us to be on our guard. The problem begins when these prophecy experts assume that everything is pointing to their present day. Naturally, once one accepts this assumption it is not too difficult to read the book of Revelation in light of current events. Indeed, it has never been too hard to make the two fit!

a nuclear blast, and the locusts with human faces (9:7) are military heli-copters. Although some of this reasoning might have an air of plausibility, there is a fundamental error in approaching the book of Revelation this way. The assumption that Revelation is about the distant future (i.e., dis-tant for John) often minimizes John's stress on the fulfillment of the OT in Jesus and usually misses completely John's consistent words of exhortation to his readers (i.e., the seven churches of Asia).

This is not to say that Revelation has nothing to do with the future—of course, it does. Revelation, after all, describes the return of Christ (19:11–16) and the final descent of the new Jerusalem (21:1–22:5).

Revelation, however, just like the prophets of the OT, and even the writings of Paul and other NT authors, is more concerned with the pres-ent. That is, John was writing to seven churches that existed at the time of his writing, and his primary concern was their faithfulness. John writes to exhort them to overcome by reminding them that in Christ God's promis-es have been fulfilled and by laying out what this means for them.

That Revelation exhorts its first-century readers to "calculate" (13:18) and to "stay awake" (16:15) means that this book must have had a meaning for its original readers. Otherwise, how could they have been blessed for "heed[ing] the things which are written in it" (1:3)?

In light of the extensive OT background for the images of Revelation, it is apparent that there is no need to jump to the future in order to provide an explanation of John's images. Instead of asserting that the imagery in Revelation is John's efforts to describe nuclear war, it makes more sense, as I have contended, that John is rereading the OT through the lens of Jesus.[2]

Does Revelation have relevance for today? Of course, it does. Revelation's importance for the people of God today is no different than Philippians. Both were written to a first-century audience. And the message of both transcends time and maintains its significance for the people of God in the present. This is not to deny that Revelation's language and imagery can make it more difficult to understand.

---

2. Some of the imagery in the book of Revelation derives from literature outside the Scriptures. Many of these are Jewish sources that were well known by the people of John's day. It is not surprising that John should include them. After all, pastors and teachers around the globe today regularly use contemporary images when proclaiming the gospel.

The Nature of Language in Scripture in General and Prophecy in Particular

One of the more common mistakes made by the popular interpreters of biblical prophecy is to impose on the biblical writers various assumptions concerning the nature of the prophetic language. The problem is that these assumptions often conflict with the nature of prophecy in the biblical world. Well-known NT scholar Gordon Fee notes:

> In my classes over the years when teaching this great book [Revelation], I make a final plea in the opening lecture regarding *the necessity of exegesis* as the proper way—indeed the *only* way—that leads to understanding. . . . The unfortunate reality is that almost all of the popular stuff written on Revelation, which tends to be well known by many of these students, has scarcely a shred of exegetical basis to it. Such interpreters usually begin with a previously worked out eschatological scheme that they bring to the text, a scheme into which they tend to spend an extraordinary amount of energy trying to make everything in the text fit, and which they then attempt to defend, but with very little success.[1]

Among such interpreters it is regularly asserted that the biblical writers used language literally. In one sense, we may all agree with this statement.

---

1. Gordon Fee, Revelation, *New Covenant Commentary*, Kindle ed. (Eugene, OR: Cascade Books, 2011), location 43. Emphasis original.

Especially since "literal" is often used as a synonym for "true." Certainly, I believe that what is being communicated in the Bible is true (hence, in that sense at least, literal). Beyond this, however, the meaning of "literal" and "literally" is ambiguous.

On the one hand, by "literal" one might mean "normal." If by saying that we should understand the words of the Bible literally one meant that we should understand the language of the prophets in particular and Scripture in general as one normally understands a typical communication, there would still be room for figurative or symbolic meanings to Scripture. After all, even in our own casual conversations, it is often difficult to discern whether or not the normal sense is figurative or whether a figurative sense instead goes beyond such normal senses of the words being used.

This was also true in the biblical world. For example, in John 11 Jesus tells His disciples that "our friend Lazarus has fallen asleep" (John 11:11). The disciples, taking Jesus' words in the non-figurative sense of "sleeping" respond, "Lord, if he has fallen asleep, he will recover" (John 11:12). John then clarifies for his readers, "Now Jesus had spoken of his death, but they thought that he was speaking of literal sleep" (John 11:13).

The same type of misunderstanding occurs in a prophetic context in John 2. There Jesus, in response to the demand for a sign, replies, "Destroy this temple, and in three days I will raise it up" (John 2:19). The Jews, however, misunderstanding Jesus, assert, "It took forty-six years to build this temple, and You will raise it up in three days?" (John 2:20). John, then, clarifies for his readers, "He was speaking of the temple of His body" (John 2:20).

The result is that literal meaning, even in the sense of "normal," is not always easily discerned. This problem is compounded by the fact that prophetic, and even more so apocalyptic, language is often used in a manner that transcends the normal. And, of course, if by "literal" we mean "non-figurative," it would seem that Scripture does indeed contain many uses of language that go beyond the literal, especially in the prophetic and apocalyptic writings just mentioned.

LITERAL INTERPRETATION?

Now some readers may be naturally apprehensive at the suggestion that prophecy may be fulfilled in a manner that transcends the literal. This is understandable. For at this point the Scriptures appear vulnerable: After all, who determines if a prophecy is to be understood in a "literal/normal" sense, or in a figurative sense? As a result, some conclude that the wisest approach is to put safeguards on the Bible, which then leads to the suggestion that the best solution is to read all Scripture in a literal sense unless the text clearly tells us otherwise.

Though this position appears to be the wise and safe one, there are a number of problems with it. The first problem is that this position represents a failure to understand that the Scriptures in general are about Jesus,[2] and that John, in particular, was writing about Jesus. John, indeed, had a message for his readers, and that message began with Jesus. If we assume that the text must always be read literally, then we must ask whether Jesus was correct when He said that He was the temple (John 2:19). Since we know that Christ was correct in His assertion, we are immediately cautioned that perhaps there is something greater happening in the biblical text that transcends the literal meaning. That something greater, of course, centers on Jesus.

Our first objective in reading Scripture, then, is to discern how the language is pointing us to Christ. When reading the book of Revelation, one does not need to conclude that because Revelation 19:12 says "and on His head are many diadems," then Jesus must actually have a bunch of crowns on His head in some literal sense. The meaning of this expression is that Jesus is the true King. It is meant to contrast Jesus with others. When others are said to have crowns on their heads, it is always a specific number of crowns. Jesus, by contrast, has "many crowns," because He is the true Lord.

Second, the assertion that the Bible must be read literally unless we are told otherwise might actually undermine the very purpose of the authors of Scripture: What if they did not want us to read something literally? Could it be that in our efforts to safeguard the Bible from misinterpretation we have ourselves misinterpreted the Bible? Would it not be better, then, to conclude that the Scriptures must be read and understood in light of what its authors intended?

---

2. I argue this extensively in both *Understanding Eschatology: Why It Matters* (Eugene, OR: Wipf & Stock, 2013), chapter 5; and *These Brothers of Mine* (Eugene, OR: Wipf & Stock, 2011), chapter 10.

In addition, what justification is there for placing such limitations on the meaning of Scripture? Where in Scripture does the Bible actually say that it must be interpreted literally unless it says otherwise? Who came up with that rule? What gives anyone the right, let alone the authority, to declare that this is the way the Bible *must* be read?[3] In other words, if the Bible never says that the proper means of interpreting it is to assume something is meant literally unless it states otherwise, then who are we to impose that rule on the Bible?

Finally, it seems as though there are many places in Scripture where the literal meaning is not the correct meaning.[4] In fact, most who believe that the Bible must be interpreted literally agree that the Bible is not to be interpreted literally at all times.[5]

This means that we should read the book of Revelation in the same manner in which we read any Scripture, namely, in light of the author's intent. Understanding the genre and the author's intent for writing is paramount.

When it comes to the book of Revelation we might conclude that Jesus does not literally have a sword coming from His mouth, though it is true that when He speaks, justice happens. At His return, Jesus will not literally be riding a white horse, though He is the returning king.

Admittedly, the interpretation of prophecy is no simple task. It is made easier, however, when we recognize that prophecy was primarily direct-ed at the people to whom it was originally written. The prophets were

---

3. What is ironic about those who advocate that the Bible must be interpreted literally is that those very same people in many cases are the most outspoken proponents of the view that the Bible is the only source of our Christian beliefs (a belief that I am not here denying). Yet when it comes to interpreting the Bible, they assert that it must be interpreted literally, something which the Bible never says. So if the Bible is the only source for Christian beliefs, then where did they come up with this conviction that the Bible must be interpreted literally?

4. Jesus is not literally a building, though He is the temple of God; neither is He a loaf of bread, though He is the source of all our sustenance. In addition, though some assert that Jesus' parables are literal, historical stories, virtually no one in the scholarly world would affirm this. The genre of parables, and the context of the Gospels, strongly confirm that Jesus was simply telling stories to illustrate a point. That story need not be historically true for His point to be valid.

5. For example, I know of no scholar that would contend that Satan is actually a seven-headed dragon.

concerned with the character and conduct of their contemporaries. The language of the Bible must be read from this perspective.

Ultimately, it is not always clear what the author meant, nor how the readers may have understood it. Thus we will have to leave room for disagreements.

REVELATION IN THE FIRST CENTURY

Though contemporary readers are often overwhelmed with the myriad of images in the book of Revelation, and are often bewildered as to what they could possibly mean, we might wonder if John's original readers would have had the same level of confusion. On several occasions, in fact, John assumes that his readers can understand and apply the message to their lives. After all, the blessing for those who "heed the things which are written in it" (Rev. 1:3) makes no sense if they cannot understand it. How could they possibly do what it says and reap the blessing that comes to those who do so, if the book only had application to some future generation and its meaning was allusive to them? And consider John's famous charge concerning the number of the beast. He exhorts his readers: "Let him who has understanding calculate the number of the beast" (13:18). This exhortation assumes that his readers were able to determine the number of the beast. After all, why exhort them to try to figure out what the number meant if they had no ability to do so?

Therefore, in order to read and understand the book of Revelation well we must first discern what the book meant to its original audience. Only then can we discern what the message might mean and how we might apply it.

Evangelicals and Armageddon

A look at the nature of holy war in the book of Revelation raises questions related to the attitude of warfare within the Western evangelical church.

First, there appears to be a dangerous tendency that arises from an overemphasis on an impending, literal battle of Armageddon.

It is my concern that one of the dangerous effects of the popular conceptions of Armageddon is complacency. The notion that Revelation describes some futuristic battle has led many to sit back comfortably and put their guard down. After all, the Armageddon of popular theology is clearly not present. This leads many to conclude that we can just sit back and relax until such events become real.

Others are driven to complacency by the conviction that when all of the apocalyptic phenomena begins they will be raptured out of the way.[1] This too can be a dangerous theology. Revelation, and the whole NT, let alone the whole of Scripture, is clear that we are at war—the devil is pursuing God's people.

> And the dragon was enraged with the woman, and went off to make war with the rest of her offspring, who keep the commandments of God and hold to the testimony of Jesus. (12:17)

---

1. I recognize that some are motivated by the conviction that Christ may soon return. This motivation drives them to evangelism. That is all well and good. But my personal experience is that many Christians in this camp become complacent. They believe that there is no need for them to do otherwise, for they suppose that they will soon be raptured up.

And he is very upset!

We see here and elsewhere that the devil is not only currently waging war on God's people, but that he is pretty angry: "For this reason, rejoice, O heavens and you who dwell in them. Woe to the earth and the sea, because the devil has come down to you, having great wrath, knowing that he has only a short time" (12:12). This means that instead of sitting back and watching the news to see if some literal, physical battle will break out in the Middle East, the people of God are called to be actively resisting the enemy.

I could preach for quite a while on this subject. After all, this is a prevalent theme in the NT. But since such a diversion would take us too far afield from our focus on the book of Revelation, I will only mention in passing Paul and James' exhortations. Paul says:

> For our struggle is not against flesh and blood, but against the rulers, against the powers, against the world forces of this darkness, against the spiritual forces of wickedness in the heavenly places. Therefore, take up the full armor of God, that you may be able to resist in the evil day, and having done everything, to stand firm. (Eph. 6:12–13)

James similarly exhorts his readers, "Submit therefore to God. Resist the devil and he will flee from you" (James 4:7).

The second dangerous error that has crept into evangelicalism over the last few years is an ardent militarism. Tragically, and quite amazingly, many Christians are so convinced that there will be a literal, final battle that takes place in the Middle East immediately prior to the return of Christ, they have actually supported war in order to facilitate the return of Christ.[2] This conviction is very common among a wide range of evangelicals.

I have argued in *Understanding Eschatology* that the NT never says that Christ will return in order to bring some literal, physical, final battle in the Middle East to an end. Instead, Christ will return to rescue

---

2. I have written on the second coming of Christ and what the NT says must happen before Christ returns in chapter 9 of *Understanding Eschatology: Why It Matters* (Eugene, OR: Wipf & Stock, 2013). As a result, I will be brief here.

His people, the church.[3] Satan's battle is not against the nations; the battle is against the people of God. We have already noticed that Revelation 12:17 says that the dragon is pursuing the people of God: "So the dragon was enraged with the woman, and went off to make war with the rest of her children, who keep the commandments of God and hold to the testimony of Jesus" (12:17). Revelation 13 affirms this when it declares, "It was also given to him to make war with the saints and to overcome them" (13:7). Throughout the book of Revelation the war is always waged by the dragon and his minions against God, Christ, and the people of God.

The common focus among some evangelicals on war in the Middle East is tragic for many reasons. Chief among them is the fact that it negates the very clear teaching of the Scriptures that Satan's war is against God's people. This means that the people of God must constantly be ready.

This is, in fact, the focus of Jesus' words to His disciples in His famed "end-times" speech (Mark 13; cf. Luke 17, 21; Matthew 24–25). He was concerned that they be prepared for the mission that they were summoned to carry out and for the opposition that they would face. Hence in Mark's Gospel, Jesus consistently warned them to "watch out" (Mark 13:5, 9, 23, 33), "do not be alarmed" (Mark 13:7), and "pray" (Mark 13:18).

In addition, there is nothing in Jesus' "end-times" speech to His disciples that would inform them of the time of His return. This, of course, makes sense in light of the fact that Jesus said that even He did not know when He was going to return! (Mark 13:32). Instead, Jesus was preparing them for their mission and for the adversity they would face as a result of this mission.

What mattered most about Jesus' return was that the disciples would be found doing His work. This corresponds to the stress throughout the NT: The people of God must be actively prepared for Christ's return by fulfilling their mission as the "light of the world." The key is that when Christ returns he finds them engaged in this very work: "Blessed is that slave whom his master finds so doing when he comes" (Matt. 24:46). Since the people of God have an enemy who will oppose their efforts, it is all the more essential for the people of God to "watch out" and "pray."

---

3. Readers are encouraged to consult *Understanding Eschatology* chapter 11 for more details.

Now, in one sense, the notion that Jesus' return will end the final battle (Armageddon) is correct. We must simply be sure that we have an accurate understanding of this final battle. The NT is clear that the final battle is that which the devil wages against Christ. The devil does so not by attacking Christ, but by attacking His people. It is not a literal, physical war waged with material weapons. Instead, it can be found anytime the devil attacks God's people.

There is a great and tragic irony with regard to the popular evangelical convictions about Armageddon. As we have seen, Armageddon is not to be construed as a literal battle between the nations of the world. It is the battle the devil wages against God's people. This battle has been waged for centuries, is being waged at this very hour, and will continue until the day Christ slays His enemies with the splendor of His coming. Christians who are waiting for some literal battle to take place in the Middle East are often unaware that they are presently in the midst of the very battle they are trying to find by watching the nightly news. They somehow have missed the very thing they are looking for.

To say it again: By looking for a literal battle in the Middle East fought between the nations such Christians have failed to see that the devil is presently waging war against them.

This explains why the book of Revelation does not depict the war itself, but only the result of the war. There is no need to provide such details—only the assurance that the people of God will one day be vindicated.[4] The result of the war in Revelation is that the beast and the false prophet and the kings of the earth are defeated by Christ (17:14; 19:15) and thrown into the lake of fire (19:20). That this is their final outcome is meant to give encouragement and hope to the people of God. In the meantime, the people of God must carry out their mission faithfully in order that they may overcome and that the nations might be counted among the great multitude.

---

4. Of course, there is no need to provide details of the final defeat of the devil and his minions because Armageddon is not a literal, physical war. In a sense, one can say that the NT and the book of Revelation do provide us with the details of this battle. After all, that is what the NT is all about. Satan will wage war against God's people. If we want specific details as to what this looks like, all we must do is study the suffering of God's people in the NT (Stephen and James' martyrdoms are recorded in the book of Acts; Paul's sufferings are recounted throughout the NT), as well as a survey of church history, and even, tragically, the daily newscasts.

It must be understood, then, that holy war in the book of Revelation (let alone the whole of Scripture) is waged against the people of God. The people of God are victorious in this war not because they take up arms and defeat their enemies, but because they love their enemies and lay down their lives as a witness to them. The people of God are pronounced victorious in the resurrection (11:11–12). This is why Revelation affirms, "Blessed are the dead who die in the Lord from now on" (14:13).

APPENDIX 4

Is Revelation about the
End of the World?

Yes and no. We have seen that the book of Revelation is about Jesus. Revelation reveals to God's people the significance of the fact that the fulfillment of God's promises to redeem the nations have begun in Jesus. He is the Lion/Lamb who has overcome. In addition, Christ is the model for the people of God. He is the "faithful and true witness" (3:14; 19:11). Therefore, follow the Lamb!

We have seen that following the Lamb means that we must persevere as faithful witnesses. And that it is through our faithfulness that God will bring about the redemption of the nations. But this comes with a strong warning: following the Lamb will not be easy. There will be much opposition to the work of God's people. Temptations will come. Suffering will come. "Hang in there," says John. "Overcome!"

The book of Revelation does take us to the end. We are reminded that there is a reward awaiting us in glory. God will create a new heavens and a new earth (21:1). So yes, the book of Revelation describes the end of the world. Specifically, it describes God's plan for redeeming the nations. This plan finds its fulfillment in Christ and continues to unfold until the end. As such, the book of Revelation describes the eternal consequences for all. Those who follow the Lamb will eat at the marriage supper of the Lamb (19:7–9) and will dwell eternally in the new Jerusalem (Revelation 21–22). Those who refuse to repent will suffer in the lake of fire (Revelation 20).

At the same time I would say, no, the book of Revelation is not about the end of the world. In doing so I have two thoughts in mind. First, it is not about the end in that the end is not the immediate focus of the book. The focus is on Christ and the work of God's people in the here and now. The book is about overcoming as the Lamb overcame. The presence of the end does convey hope to the people of God. This, however, is not the *focus* of the book of Revelation.

Second, it is not about the end of the world in that it in no way gives us hints or insights into the timing of the end. Many Christians have the conception that Revelation describes the future and provides a sort of road map as to when and how everything ends. It is in this sense that I would say emphatically that the book of Revelation is not about the end. The focus in the NT as a whole, and the book of Revelation in particular, is on the faithful, persevering witness of God's people.

As referenced earlier, this is similar to Jesus' speech on the "end-times" in Mark 13. Jesus' disciples ask Him when all these things would happen. A simple look at Jesus' reply confirms that he was focused not on *when* He was to return, but on *how* they were to live in the meantime. This is clear from the numerous exhortations in Jesus' reply: "See to it that no one misleads you" (Mark 13:5); "be on your guard" (Mark 13:9); "do not worry" (Mark 13:11); "the one who endures to the end, he will be saved" (Mark 13:13); "but when you see . . . flee to the mountains" (Mark 13:14); "but pray" (Mark 13:18); "if anyone says to you . . . do not believe him" (Mark 13:21); "take heed" (Mark 13:23); "when you see . . . recognize" (Mark 13:29); "take heed, keep on the alert, for you do not know" (Mark 13:33); "be on the alert—for you do not know" (Mark 13:35); "what I say to you I say to all, be on the alert" (Mark 13:37).

As is clearly evident, the message of Christ to His disciples was focused not on when these things would happen, but on their faithfulness in the midst of it all.

The book of Revelation opens with a blessing for its readers, hearers, and keepers (1:3). As much as we want to know how it will all unfold, the message of Scripture is far more concerned with how we live in the present than with what we know about the future. If we spend too much time debating end-times scenarios, and fail to fully grasp the message of the book of Revelation, and the whole of Scripture for that matter, and its application to our lives, then the dragon wins, the kingdom of God does not come, and the people of God will fail to receive the very blessing for which the book was composed.

Bibliography

This annotated bibliography is provided to assist the reader as you continue in your studies in the book of Revelation.

Aune, David E. *Revelation*. Word Biblical Commentary 52A–C. Dallas: Word Books, 1996–98. Good resources for the serious student. A bit outdated now.

Bauckham, Richard. *The Climax of Prophecy: Studies on the Book of Revelation*. Edinburgh: T&T Clark, 1993. A must-read for the serious student. Knowledge of Greek is necessary.

_____. *The Theology of the Book of Revelation*. Cambridge: Cambridge University Press, 1993.

Beale, Gregory K. *The Book of Revelation: A Commentary on the Greek Text*. New International Greek Testament Commentary. Grand Rapids: Eerdmans, 1999. One of the standard-bearers of the study of Revelation. Exhaustive. Excellent for graduate students.

_____. *John's Use of the Old Testament in Revelation*. Sheffield: Sheffield Academic Press, 1998. Very helpful for the serious student.

Boettner, Loraine. *The Millennium*. Philadelphia: Presbyterian and Reformed, 1957. An introduction to four views.

Caird, George Bradford. *A Commentary on the Revelation of St. John the Divine*. Harper's New Testament Commentary. New York: Harper, 1966.

Chilton, David. *The Days of Vengeance: An Exposition of the Book of Revelation*. Fort Worth: Dominion, 1986. Views Revelation from the perspective that much in Revelation relates to the destruction of Jerusalem in AD 70.

Clouse, Robert G., ed. *The Meaning of the Millennium: Four Views.* Downers Grove, IL: InterVarsity Press, 1977. The four main views of the millennium are presented by proponents of each view, represented by George Ladd, Herman Hoyt, Loraine Boettner, and Anthony Hoekema. Each scholar presents his view and responds to the other presentations.

Colclasure, Chuck. *The Overcomers: The Unveiling of Hope, Comfort, and Encouragement in the Book of Revelation.* Nashville: Nelson, 1981.

Dalrymple, Rob. *Understanding Eschatology: Why It Matters.* Eugene, OR: Wipf & Stock, 2013. Argues that the end-times began with the arrival of the kingdom of God and the first coming of Jesus. Very helpful for those wanting to understand the end-times from a biblical perspective. Accessible to all readers.

_____. *Revelation and the Two Witnesses.* Eugene, OR: Wipf & Stock, 2011. Advanced look at the people of God in Revelation 11.

_____. "The Use of *kai*, in Revelation 11,1 and the Implications for the Identification of the Temple, the Altar, and the Worshipers." *Biblica* 87 (2006): 387–94.

_____. "These Are the Ones . . . (Rev 7)." *Biblica* 86 (2005): 396–406.

_____. *These Brothers of Mine: A Biblical Theology of Land and Family and a Biblical Response to Christian Zionism.* Eugene, OR: Wipf & Stock, 2011.

deSilva, David A. *Unholy Allegiances: Heeding Revelation's Warning.* Peabody, MA: Hendrickson, 2013. Very good.

_____. *Seeing Things John's Way: The Rhetoric of the Book of Revelation.* Louisville: Westminster John Knox Press, 2009. Very good. Advanced.

Ezell, Douglas. *Revelations on Revelation: New Sounds from Old Symbols.* Waco, TX: Word, 1977. Helpful for understanding apocalyptic.

Fee, Gordon. *Revelation.* New Covenant Commentary. Kindle Edition. Eugene, OR: Cascade Books, 2011.

Gentry, Kenneth L., Jr. *Before Jerusalem Fell: Dating the Book of Revelation.* Fort Worth: Dominion Press, 1989. Views Revelation from the position that the book was written prior to AD 70.

Goldsworthy, Graeme. *The Lamb and the Lion: The Gospel in Revelation.* Nashville: Thomas Nelson, 1985. A very good, lay-level introduction to Revelation.

Gorman, Michael. *Reading Revelation Responsibly: Uncivil Worship and Witness—Following the Lamb into the New Creation*. Eugene, OR: Wipf & Stock, 2011. Excellent resource. Very insightful on applying the book of Revelation to various contemporary issues.

Hemer, Colin J. *The Letters to the Seven Churches of Asia in Their Local Setting*. Grand Rapids: Eerdmans, 2000. An introduction on the historical background of the seven churches.

Hendrickson, William. *More than Conquerors: An Interpretation of the Book of Revelation*. Grand Rapids: Baker, 1961. An excellent resource and readable for the lay person.

Hoekema, Anthony. *The Bible and the Future*. Grand Rapids: Eerdmans, 1979.

Keener, Craig S. *Revelation*. NIV Application Commentary. Grand Rapids: Zondervan, 2000. Excellent and fairly easy to read. Great starting place for most readers wanting to go deeper.

Kraybill, J. Nelson. *Apocalypse and Allegiance*. Grand Rapids: Brazos Press, 2010. Very good.

Ladd, George Eldon. *A Commentary on the Revelation of John*. Grand Rapids: Eerdmans, 1972.

Longman, Tremper, III. "The Divine Warrior: The New Testament Use of an Old Testament Motif." *Westminster Theological Journal* 44 (1982): 290–307.

Metzger, Bruce M. *Breaking the Code: Understanding the Book of Revelation*. Nashville: Abingdon, 1993.

Michaels, J. Ramsey. *Interpreting the Book of Revelation*. Guides to New Testament Exegesis. Grand Rapids: Baker, 1998.

Minear, Paul S. *I Saw a New Earth: An Introduction to the Visions of the Apocalypse*. Eugene, OR: Wipf & Stock, 2003.

Morris, Leon. *The Revelation of St. John: An Introduction and Commentary*. Tyndale New Testament Commentaries. London: Tyndale, 1969.

Mounce, Robert H. *What Are We Waiting For? Commentary on Revelation*. Grand Rapids: Eerdmans, 1992. Introductory commentary.

_____. *The Book of Revelation*. New International Commentary on the New Testament. Grand Rapids: Eerdmans, 1977. A great place to start for those wanting to go deeper.

Moyise, Steve. *The Old Testament in the Book of Revelation*. Sheffield: Sheffield Academic Press, 1995.

Osborne, Grant R. *Revelation*. Baker Exegetical Commentary on the New Testament. Grand Rapids: Baker, 2002.

Peterson, Eugene H. *Reversed Thunder: The Revelation of John and the Praying Imagination*. San Francisco: Harper & Row, 1988. A great place to start for those wanting to go deeper.

Poythress, Vern S. *The Returning King: A Guide to the Book of Revelation*. Phillipsburg, NJ: Presbyterian & Reformed, 2000. Very simple yet insightful. Good place for the beginner to start.

Poythress, Vern S. "Counterfeiting in the Book of Revelation as a Perspective on Non-Christian Culture." *Journal of the Evangelical Theological Society* 40, no. 3 (1997): 411–18.

Ramsay, William M. *The Letters of the Seven Churches of Asia*. New York: Armstrong, 1905. Very good historical archaeological study.

Resseguie, James L. *The Revelation of John: A Narrative Commentary*. Grand Rapids: Baker, 2009.

Rossing, Barbara. *The Rapture Exposed: The Message of Hope in the Book of Revelation*. New York: Basic Books, 2009.

Ryken, Leland. "Revelation." In *A Complete Literary Guide to the Bible,* edited by Leland Ryken and Tremper Longman III, 458–69. Grand Rapids: Zondervan, 1993.

Sandy, Brent. *Plowshares and Pruning Hooks: Rethinking the Language of Biblical Prophecy and Apocalyptic*. Downers Grove, IL: InterVarsity Press, 2002.

Smalley, Stephen S. *The Revelation to John: A Commentary on the Greek Text of the Apocalypse*. Downers Grove, IL: InterVarsity Press, 2005.

Stott, John. *Revelation: The Triumph of Christ*. Downers Grove, IL: InterVarsity Press, 2008.

Strand, Kenneth A. *Interpreting the Book of Revelation: Hermeneutical Guidelines, with Brief Introduction to Literary Analysis*. Worthington, OH: Ann Arbor Press, 1976.

Tenney, Merrill C. *Interpreting Revelation*. Grand Rapids: Eerdmans, 1957.

Thomas, Derek. *Let's Study Revelation*. Carlyle, PA: Banner of Truth, 2003.

Wilcock, Michael. *I Saw Heaven Opened: The Message of Revelation*. Downers Grove, IL: InterVarsity Press, 1975.

Wilson, Mark. *Charts on the Book of Revelation: Literary, Historical, and Theological Perspectives*. Grand Rapids: Kregel, 2007.